Look at the Birds of the Air

Lessons from birds in the Bible

Mark Winter

Illustrations by Simon Terry

For Sheila, my wife and dearest friend

Contents

Introduction

> *Look at the birds of the air; they do not sow or reap or store away in barns, and yet your heavenly Father feeds them. Are you not much more valuable than they?*
>
> Matthew 6 verse 26

Jesus told his followers to look at the birds of the air. Look at the birds and learn about God's generous provision. He explained that if God provides so well for the material needs of birds, then people should not worry about food or clothing and instead trust in God's loving care for them. That message of Jesus applies to us as well. As twenty-first century followers, we too are taught by Jesus to look at the birds and learn. We too should learn to trust in a heavenly father who cares for our needs as any loving parent would.

People learning from birds about God was not an idea unique to Jesus. His teaching followed a rich Jewish tradition going back to Moses, and evident throughout the Old Testament, of people observing birds and drawing lessons about God's character and purposes. Moses sang of God being like a parent eagle catching its young to prevent them falling. The psalmists spoke of the Lord protecting them like a bird with wings. Prophets like Isaiah, Jeremiah and Ezekiel repeatedly used bird imagery to proclaim what God was doing. And the wisdom literature of Proverbs and Job made many references to birds. Over the centuries people in Israel observed avian phenomena such as bird migration or birds feeding on carrion, interpreted them as metaphors and drew lessons about God's care for humanity alongside the rest of creation. Delve into the pages of the Bible and you will find a multitude of references to birds. Some relate to particular types of birds and others to birds in general. Some describe what birds do and others to what can happen to them, usually as a result of human activity. Specific birds feature in the narratives of prominent individuals like Noah, Abraham, Elijah, Peter and of course Jesus himself. Strange forms of birds appear in the dreams and visions of prophets like Ezekiel and Daniel, while other prophets warn of birds acting as agents of divine judgement on Israel's rulers and people. Laws are given for their protection and regulations for their ritual slaughter. Birds feature in prophecy and poetry, wise sayings and songs of worship, even in the intimate conversation of two lovers.

This book has a simple message. We should 'look at the birds of the air', consider their circumstances of God-given sufficiency and recognise that we too have enough for our needs from a loving father in heaven. Jesus gave a straightforward command and it's easy to follow. When you go outside, glance around you and look at the birds.

My Story of Watching Birds

I have been looking at birds for over fifty years. Perversely, it all started for me when I didn't look at a bird because I wasn't there to see it. When I was only seven years old, my parents and young sister saw an unusual bird feeding on berries in our garden in Maidstone, Kent. They told me about it when I returned from school and my interest was kindled. I was disappointed that I hadn't seen it and I was intrigued to find out more. The bird in question was a Waxwing - a pink bird the size of a Starling with a distinctive crest and wings attractively edged with black, white and wax-yellow. In that winter of 1966 Britain saw a huge influx of these beautiful visitors from northern Russia and Scandinavia, coming here for our milder winter climate and relative abundance of berries. Many older birdwatchers still remember that year for the 'Waxwing invasion' when tens of thousands wintered here.

Not long afterwards my family moved to the countryside to

live in a vicarage with a large garden and a wonderful variety of trees. We had plenty of birds to see and hear including the Blackbird that sang regularly outside our kitchen window, prompting my mother to feed him. Mr Cunningham, a teacher at the village primary school, fostered my emerging interest and I saved enough pocket money to buy my first pair of binoculars - a cheap pair of 7 x 50 East German Zeiss. They were optically sharp and my prize possession. I joined the Young Ornithologists Club, paired up with a local adult RSPB member and went out on field trips with him and a couple of other boys to special locations for birds like Dungeness and the north Kent marshes. I ventured further afield on family holidays when we would each be allowed one day to choose the itinerary - funfair for my sister, town shopping for my mum, gardens for my dad and a birdwatching day for me. I wouldn't necessarily inflict the birding ordeal on the three of them, providing I could be dropped off and collected at an agreed time. It was a different age with much less apparent concern about child safety. Hence I went to Lundy Island for the day birdwatching in the company of strangers that we had met queuing for the ferry. Aged ten and alone I spent a morning wandering around a Dorset heath, successfully tracking down an elusive Dartford Warbler. All exciting stuff for a pre-adolescent nerd in an anorak to match. I spent many hours watching birds, reading about them and drawing them from books, although I didn't develop any artistic skills as a consequence. However, I had some pretensions as a child poet and wrote a poem about my hobby.

BIRDWATCHING

It was from that it started.
It led me into a new world.
A world of birds.
A world of Lundy, Fetlar, Fair Isle, St Kilda.
A world of excitement and disappointment.
From the gannet, diving in the sea,
To the treecreeper, running up a tree.
From the zigzag flying snipe
To the high soaring swift.
It is a world of magnificence and splendour,
A world of solo and duet.
Yet I wonder would I give it up,
Just because I might see
The bird I have never seen

by Mark Winter (aged 11)

Eventually I saw my first Waxwing when I was seventeen, but I didn't give up birdwatching. I chose York University to do my undergraduate degree because of a bird – seeing a Kingfisher at the campus on my applicant visit and taking it as a sign, although I never saw another during the three years I studied there.

In 1983 I moved to North-East England to work for Traidcraft, the Christian firm set up to promote fairer trade with the world's poor. One of my bosses introduced me to a birdwatcher in his church, and I soon became good friends with Geoffrey Peter Bull. Pete was a truly outstanding birder with a brilliant ability for spotting unusual birds, as well as having considerable flair as an amateur taxidermist. Over a fifteen-year period Pete and I frequently went out birdwatching. Most of our trips were local, visiting sites around Newcastle like Swallow Pond, St Mary's Island and Newbiggen golf course – one of the best migration hotspots locally where we found our share of migrant rarities blown in on easterly winds: Icterine Warbler; Siberian Stonechat; Rough-legged Buzzard. We joined forces with a handful of Pete's work colleagues for a long weekend in Norfolk each May – a secular pilgrimage when we ritually visited a series of special birding 'hotspots' like Cley and Blakeney Point. We did our annual catch-up with East Anglian breeding birds rarely seen at home: Stone Curlew and Woodlark on the heathland of the Brecks; Golden Oriole and Lesser Spotted Woodpecker in the Black Poplar plantations; and Avocets, Bearded Tits and Bitterns on the north Norfolk coastal marshes. We also followed whatever 'news' we could glean about rare birds in the area, and over the years we saw an impressive range of vagrant birds like the Oriental Pratincole from China or the Lark Sparrow from North America.

We usually denied being 'twitchers' – the obsessive birdwatchers who might drive great distances to see rare birds – yet on that annual jaunt we somehow made an exception for ourselves. Going to Norfolk was a trip that we anticipated with relish for weeks beforehand, but on one memorable occasion we travelled in the opposite direction northwards to the Scottish Highlands. Memorable because of a very close encounter with a rogue male Capercaillie that chased us along a path in Abernethy Forest. Close enough for him to bite Pete! The bird eventually lost interest in chasing us and he wandered off to graze on bilberries while we sat down nearby and watched him in amazement. What a wonderful memory that I still treasure. Pete's untimely death in Millennium Year at the age of forty three was an extremely sad loss for his family and friends, and it hit me hard in losing not only a close friend, but also my birding partner.

Back in October 1994 Pete and I organised a weekend on Holy Island for some Christian friends to show them the birds. It proved great fun and the idea was born of us offering bird guiding. We didn't pursue it further, but after Pete's death some of those friends asked me to take them birdwatching again. I followed up by starting a micro-business as a bird guide, and in November 2004 I organised and co-led a weekend retreat on Holy Island, combining the watching of birds with Christian worship and reflection on birds. It was the first of many such retreats in Northumberland. Various friends have helped along the way, notably the Reverend Adrian Hughes whom I first met on Holy Island watching a Greenish Warbler.

I still enjoy watching birds. I don't go out every day to watch despite being retired, yet I am always watching and listening out for birds wherever I am and have my binoculars close to hand. I don't obsess about lists, but I keep a garden list (ninety six species by March 2018), an annual list, a UK tally and a list for the old county of Northumberland, north of the Tyne. That fourth list is the one of most importance to me and I take some pride in its current total of three hundred and thirty four species.

People often ask me what's my favourite bird and frankly I don't have one. Given how I started, I still love seeing

Waxwings and I have now seen hundreds, as well as owning a stuffed one which resides in my study. (For the record, it died of natural causes, lest anyone think I caused its death in order to possess a 'specimen'!) Yet I also especially enjoy watching tiny warblers and powerful raptors – two kinds of birds that contrast starkly. I enjoy the fresh appeal of seeing birds in other countries and usually manage a birding trip to continental Europe most years – France, Spain, Portugal or Poland. Perhaps above all, I love the buzz of autumn in Northumberland when the winds swing to the east and anything can blow in from the continent. To witness a 'happening' in October with thousands of winter thrushes arriving at the coast is exhilarating. I find it a highlight to watch a Redwing flying towards the shore low over the waves and safely land on solid ground. The first dry land this small bird has seen since leaving Scandinavia many hours earlier. The Redwing looks exhausted as it silently sits on the shoreland turf. Yet moments later it flies off and calls as it heads inland. I imagine it saying "Hooray, I've made it across the North Sea," and smile.

Why I Wrote This Book

Throughout my adult life I have tried to relate my Christian faith to my interests as well as my actions. I have always understood that the birds I enjoy watching are living beings like us, created by God. Coming from an evangelical Anglican tradition, I knew about the late John Stott and read his book, *The Birds Our Teachers*. His comments on 'orni-theology' resonated with me and were a factor prompting me to organise the birdwatching retreats. Yet I wanted to go deeper and carry out my own research, exploring precisely what the Bible says about birds. In 2013 I began systematically reading through each book in the Bible and recording every verse that mentioned birds. I was keen to know which kinds of birds feature the most, how they are mentioned and in what contexts. I also sought to find out which biblical books contained the most references to birds. Above all I wanted to discover which particular birds appear in the life of Jesus, as well as the kinds he chose to mention in his teachings.

Some of my findings surprised me. I had expected to read about eagles, doves and ravens, but I didn't anticipate so many references in the Bible to chickens and owls. I didn't realise how widely these avian references are distributed across scripture, being found in twenty seven books in the Old Testament and nine books in the New. Nor did I realise the sheer variety of metaphors and associations used by biblical authors. I had known something about the teachings of Jesus regarding birds, but my research has also meant 'unlearning' previous assumptions I had made, notably about the dove's appearance when Jesus was baptised and his lack of mention of eagles.

This book is an outcome of that research journey. I have written it for others who want to know about birds in the Bible. Many wouldn't describe themselves as birdwatchers. On my retreats some people are quick to tell me how little they know about birds or indeed other aspects of wildlife. Yet they suspect there should be a connection between the Christian faith and their appreciation of nature. If you share that sense of linkage, I think this book is for you. Look at the birds, and indeed all living creatures, and learn.

My Use of The Bible

I should also explain how I try to interpret biblical text. I believe the Bible to contain the inspired and authoritative written word of God.[1] Hence I start by taking a biblical passage at face value and seek to understand its plain meaning, unless the text is obviously intended to be symbolic, poetic or hyperbole. I don't look automatically for natural explanations of events that the biblical writer clearly intended should be perceived as supernatural or miraculous, for example the 'burning bush' seen by Moses. The case of Elijah and the ravens is a pertinent example. The writer(s) of 1 Kings chapter 17 state that ravens brought bread and meat for the prophet twice daily. A situation clearly presented by the writer(s) as God miraculously providing food fit for a king for the man of God during a severe drought when he was hiding in exile from an evil king. Having been fed by God in this way, Elijah was then directed to stay with a foreign widow and be the means of providing food miraculously for her family. Commentators who argue for a natural explanation in claiming that Elijah survived by sharing in the food that the ravens brought their nestlings miss the point of the symbolism.

For the sake of consistency all the Biblical references quoted in this book come from one source. I have used the 2011 edition of the *New International Version Study Bible* (NIV). It's the one I use for personal devotion and I trust the quality of its scholarly underpinning. The first NIV Bible was published by a team of evangelical scholars in 1978 and revised in both 1985 and 2002. There are variations between some versions of the Bible in the identification of particular birds, primarily in the parallel lists of birds deemed 'unclean' found in Leviticus and Deuteronomy as I discuss in chapter 7. In my view the NIV generally has the advantage of being based on current biblical scholarship.

A Word About Bird Taxonomy

You might notice in this book that I generally avoid scientific terms for classifying birds. I write about birds being of different 'kinds' and 'types', whereas avian scientists currently use terms like 'Order', 'Family' and 'Genus'. All birds are grouped together into a single 'Class' which is then divided into various 'orders' and subdivided sequentially into 'families', 'subfamilies', 'genera' and 'species'.

Let's consider what these distinctions mean for some of the main birds we find in the Bible like the owl, dove, eagle and raven. All owls belong to a single order *Strigiformes*. It is divided into two families, *Tytonidae* that comprise barn owls, and *Strigidae* for other owls. By comparison, pigeons and doves together comprise a single family, *Columbidae*, which belongs to the order *Columbiformes*. Eagles provide further contrast as they form only one strand of the *Accipitridae* family, along with kites, buzzards, hawks and vultures. Ravens belong to the *Corvidae* family; one of many belonging to the order of perching birds, *Passiformes*, which contains over five thousand living species of bird. That multitude of species in a single order contrasts starkly with the paucity of different birds belonging to the order of flightless birds *Struthioniformes* which has only fifteen or so species including the ostrich.

How This Book is Structured

Birds are found throughout the Bible, but some kinds of birds are mentioned much more than others. Five kinds of bird feature the most. The pigeon-dove, the eagle, the chicken, the owl and the raven each have double-digit scriptural references, and each is the subject of a separate chapter in this book. A further eighteen specific kinds of birds are also identified in the Bible and these are examined together in chapter 7. In addition, there are plenty of references to unspecified birds, to birds in general, to bird anatomy and to human treatment of birds - all the subject of chapter 8. The final chapter concludes by considering one apparently insignificant 'little brown job' which we today observe around us across the world, a bird which Jesus singled out for special mention.

Chapters 2-6 form the core of this book and they adopt

the same format. Each has an introductory paragraph and five headed sections as follows:

Profile
Short description of this kind of bird. It provides material about its appearance, voice and behaviour. It also includes brief information about its current status in modern Israel – the geographical heartland of the 'Bible Lands'.

Folklore
The bird's importance in folklore, mythology, custom and cultures around the world.

My encounters
Describes my own experiences of observing the bird. I don't make any claims that these have any particular or wider significance, but I simply include them as they might parallel the experiences of some readers who find them to be of personal interest.

Bible References
Lists all the biblical references that I have found for the bird type being discussed and provides some commentary on these references. In each case it's by far the longest section. These references are also presented as one complete list at the end of the book.

Questions to Consider
A quartet of questions based on the chapter. They stem

primarily from the biblical material, but there are also some questions arising from the section on folklore.

Each chapter could be used for a bible study, structured around the four questions which I hope that you find to be thought-provoking. Perhaps you could make these five chapters the basis of a weekly course during Lent. Or you might consider them for personal study if you are exploring wider issues associated with creation care. However you choose to use them, please take some time to think about these questions and let me know your views.

The Pigeon-Dove

Does any other bird arouse such mixed emotions? Mention the word 'dove' and people think of love, peace, gentleness and purity - all positive images of birds cherished by many people. Mention the word 'pigeon' and a very different set of images may come to mind: noisy, dirty, numerous and grey ... "flying rats" to paraphrase the film producer Woody Allen. Yet doves and pigeons are one and the same kind of bird as members of the *Columbidae* bird family. The word 'pigeon' is more associated with larger family species and 'dove' with the smaller, but this association breaks down as soon as the feral pigeon is considered. This bird is our archetypal pigeon that we associate with modern cities in Europe and it's the domestic form of the cliff dwelling Rock Dove. In Britain we have both the feral birds in our urban centres and purely wild birds found among the cliffs of North-West Scotland, but they share the same DNA and are virtually impossible to tell apart. Given this shared identity, it is more appropriate to use the umbrella term 'pigeon-dove' for much of our discussion of pigeons and doves in this chapter.

Pigeon-Doves in Profile

Today there are about three hundred species of doves and pigeons across the globe, and their distribution is truly cosmopolitan. They are found in every continent except Antarctica with the greatest concentration being in South-East Asia where sixty two species can be found. Most pigeon and dove species around the world are woodland-based and eat a wide mix of grains, seeds and berries. Although they range considerably in size, they can be typically described as medium-sized with compact plump bodies that contrast to their small heads, short necks and longish tails. Most species are strong fliers – one of the main reasons for their domestication as birds historically bred for carrying messages and still bred today for racing. However, they do not soar effortlessly on thermals, but they can glide and often do so as part of their breeding displays. They can perch on tree branches as their feet typically have three front toes and a large hind toe. When they walk on the ground, they have a head 'bobbing' action. Unlike other birds they can drink with lowered bills as they suck up water. Also, unlike most other birds they can feed their young on a 'milk' - a nutritious secretion produced by their bodies. This 'pigeon milk' is secreted from the lining of the bird's relatively large crop - an expandable part of its digestive tract located just below its throat that can be used to store food temporarily.

In terms of voice, pigeons and doves make soft sounds. They typically 'coo' and 'purr'. Although there are significant variations between the species, their vocalisations can generally be described as lower pitched, repetitive and often monotonous. Indeed, the *Collins Bird Guide* uses the word "moaning" to describe the voices of the Rock Dove and Feral Pigeon.

Fecundity is another unusual attribute of doves and pigeons. Many of their species breed throughout the calendar year and can have up to six breeding cycles during it. In Britain I have found freshly discarded egg shells from local Woodpigeons in December, presumably removed from the nest by parent birds after hatching. Generally, it seems doves and pigeons pair for life and both sexes share aspects of the nesting duties including incubation. However, it also seems that both males and females proactively indulge in sexual behaviour with other pigeons - a fact known for centuries in Arab cultures with the sport of 'thief pigeons'.[2]

Finally, let's consider the identity and variety of pigeon-dove species found in the Bible Lands today. We cannot necessarily presume that any of these species lived in the region in the period of the biblical era upto and including the ministry of Jesus. We also face a second difficulty. The geography of the 'Bible

Lands' is considerably greater than Israel today. Conventionally it includes the Palestinian territories, Lebanon, Jordan, Syria, eastern Egypt, most of Turkey and much of Greece, especially when the missionary journeys of Paul are taken into account. However, I am choosing the narrow focus of modern Israel – the setting for most of the biblical references about doves and pigeons. Israel today is home to seven species of dove and pigeon, and a further two rarities are recorded on the national checklist maintained by the Israeli rarities committee.[3] The full list is as follows: Rock Dove (resident and common); Stock Dove (winter migrant); Wood Pigeon (winter migrant); Eurasian Collared Dove (resident and common); European Turtle Dove (summer migrant); Laughing Dove (resident and common); Namaqua Dove (resident but uncommon); African Collared Dove (rare winter vagrant); Oriental Turtle Dove (very rare vagrant).

Pigeon-Doves in Folklore

Let's begin with love. The pigeon-dove's combination of fecundity and monogamy has given rise to plenty of historic mythology and folklore about its love life, dating back several millennia. The ancient Babylonians, Phoenicians, Greeks and Romans associated doves with love and fertility through their deities. For example, the Greek goddess of love, Aphrodite, who was drawn in her chariot by several doves as she rode through the clouds. Today doves are associated with romantic love and their images adorn many a Valentine's or wedding card.

The other main folklore association with doves derives from the Judeo-Christian tradition, drawing imagery, if not necessarily substance, from the story of Noah's ark. The picture of a dove holding an olive branch in its beak has become an emblem of peace across today's world, irrespective of national culture. Witness the dove logo of the annual United Nations World Peace Day.

Little wonder that there are myriad myths and folktales about pigeons and doves as they are one of our oldest domesticated birds. People kept them both in ancient Egypt and in Mesopotamia. Over the centuries many millions have been slaughtered for religious sacrifice across different cultures and for eating as a source of meat protein. People designed 'dovecotes' to house them, sometimes in large numbers like the 1500 nests in the Willington dovecote near Bedford in England.[4]

Taking advantage of their homing instinct, people have also kept large numbers alive to act as message carriers, a practice dating back to the Egyptian pharaohs and maintained as recently as World War II. In addition, working class men in Europe have bred them for racing, such as the coal miners in North-East England. Although this pastime may be declining in twenty-first century Britain, it is apparently finding new enthusiasts in China, Eastern Europe and the Middle East.

A dove may be a pigeon by any other name, but the associations we make with each word contrast starkly. The malign usage of the word 'pigeon' is reflected in our English vocabulary. For example, the word itself is a synonym for dupe.

Being 'pigeon-livered' is to be cowardly - a term used by Shakespeare in Hamlet. People who are 'pigeon-toed' have a foot deformity as their feet point inward. Contrast all that to the word 'dove' - a term of endearment as well as a famous toiletry brand. No one to my knowledge has launched a soap called 'Pigeon'!

My Encounters with Pigeon-Doves

Five of the species of pigeon-doves found in modern Israel are also found as breeding birds in the UK. I have seen all five in Northumberland where I now live, but that's little cause to boast as four are common, easy to see and indeed are on my garden list. Woodpigeons are currently one of the commonest and most widespread species across Britain. They breed in my garden most of the year, and I have heard their cooing songs nearly every month. Putting out birdseed on our lawn in winter can readily attract a dozen birds, but in the fields and woods around my village there are flocks of several hundred birds much of the year. I readily admit that I also enjoy the taste of Woodpigeon and I have considered whether the plump birds feeding on my lawn would be good for the pot, but thankfully for these birds I have done nothing about it!

Collared Doves are also found in my garden and eat our birdseed. However, my strongest memories of them date from my childhood in Kent when they were irritatingly constant vocalists as they sang their three note cooing song seemingly all day long. While I don't care for their melody, I find Collared Doves attractive to look at because of their elongated shape and subtle pale buff-grey plumage. I cannot claim the same for the feral Rock Doves that usually fly over the garden but rarely land. Those that do land are, often as not, tired and apparently disoriented racing pigeons. Yet I have also seen the nearest we have to the pure form of Rock Dove on the Isle of Lewis and there was a contrast. Those birds seemed to have paler grey, more uniform and 'cleaner' plumage, and their white rumps were clearly distinctive. The fourth of my garden quartet is the Stock Dove - an infrequent visitor as a 'fly over'. I think they can be elusive and in my experience rarely heard, but these days I am noticing them more frequently. I now make the effort to check each flock of Woodpigeons as I sometimes find a handful of these doves associating with their bigger 'cousins'.

Pride of place for me goes to the Turtle Dove, sadly a rare sight across northern Britain and indeed the whole of the UK. I grew up with them in Kent where I saw and heard my first at Stodmarsh. The purring song is distinctive and reminds me of an old-fashioned telephone, but I never hear it in Northumberland. Indeed, it's a bird I have seen only once up here and I remember it well. On 28 September 2013 I was birdwatching with Adrian Hughes on Holy Island looking for autumn migrants when we found a juvenile Turtle Dove. We could see the bird was agitated as it struggled to dislodge piri-piri burr that was attached to its tail. Initially we feared for its survival as it seemed unable to fly, but eventually the bird pulled off enough burr to fly away. It was a poignant encounter - seeing an endangered bird (partly due to human hunting along its Mediterranean migration paths) succumbing to an 'alien' and invasive plant that was accidentally introduced along the Northumbrian coast nearly a century ago. It seemed like a parable as a reminder of how pernicious humankind can be to birds and other creatures, even when we don't intend it.

Pigeon-Doves in The Bible

Doves and pigeons feature much more in the Bible than any other kind of bird. In total there are thirty eight explicit references in fourteen books, and these are listed below. As this lengthy list reveals, doves and pigeons are featured across a diverse range of scripture: Genesis, the Law of Moses, Psalms, the Song of Songs, several of the Prophets and all four Gospels.

GENESIS	chapter 8 verses 8-12
	chapter 15 verses 9-11
LEVITICUS	chapter 1 verses 14-17
	chapter 5 verses 7-11
	chapter 12 verses 6-8
	chapter 14 verses 22, 30-31
	chapter 15 verses 14-15, 29
NUMBERS	chapter 6 verse 10
PSALMS	55 verse 6
	56 introduction

LUKE   chapter 2 verse 24
                             chapter 3 verses 21–22

JOHN   chapter 1 verse 32
                             chapter 2 verses 14, 16

Just like the emotions they arouse today, doves and pigeons in these biblical references present stark, contrasting images relating to their association and symbolism. They are symbols of purity or creatures for sacrifice or even objects of scorn. They demonstrated knowledge to the prophet Jeremiah, but stupidity to the prophet Hosea. They symbolised courtship to the writer of Song of Songs who associated them with sexual attraction and love, but both the prophets Isaiah and Nahum spoke dismissively of their 'moaning'. Yet above all, the dove symbolises the very presence of God – the person of the Holy Spirit. What an honour for any creature, let alone a bird!

No other bird in scripture is mentioned for sacrifice. Doves and pigeons are unique in the Bible as being birds deemed 'acceptable' for religious sacrifice to God – a practice dating back at least four thousand years when Abram sacrificed a dove and a young pigeon alongside three animals in response to a vision in which God promised him innumerable descendants (see Genesis 15). Nearly one fifth of all biblical texts about doves and pigeons can be found in the book of Leviticus with seven references to avian sacrifice regulations, mainly relating to rites of purification as means of dealing with human sin. These references give detailed instructions about the circumstances and methods of sacrifice, and they include this detail concerning sin offerings in chapter 5:

Anyone who cannot afford a lamb is to bring two doves or two young pigeons to the Lord as a penalty for their sin - one for a sin offering and the other for a burnt offering. They are to bring them to the priest, who shall first offer the one for the sin offering. He is to wring its head from its neck, not dividing it completely, and is to splash some of the blood of the sin offering against the side of the altar; the rest of the blood must be drained out at the base of the altar. It is a sin offering. The priest shall then offer the other as a burnt offering in the prescribed way and make atonement for them for the sin they have committed, and they will be forgiven.

It is interesting to note that these birds were an acceptable substitute for people too poor to afford sacrificing a lamb - the very situation faced by Joseph and Mary many centuries later when they took the infant Jesus to the temple in Jerusalem as we shall see.

Nowhere in the Bible is a reason given for doves and pigeons being selected as the one and only type of bird acceptable for sacrifice. Nor is any explanation provided about the differences between 'doves' and 'young pigeons'; presumably the latter were fledgling pigeon squabs, but we are not told. Two natural attributes clearly made them an obvious choice - their domesticated docility and their fecundity. Contrast that first attribute with the typical behaviour, say, of small falcons. Birds with hooked beaks and sharp talons, however small, would doubtless offer more resistance to a priest tasked with wringing their necks as described in Leviticus 1:

If the offering to the Lord is a burnt offering of birds, you are to offer a dove or a young pigeon. The priest shall bring it to the altar, wring off the head and burn it on the altar; its blood shall be drained out on the side of the altar. He is to remove the crop and the feathers and throw them down east of the altar where the ashes are. He shall tear it open by the wings, not dividing it completely, and then the priest shall burn it on the wood that is burning on the altar. It is a burnt offering, a food offering, an aroma pleasing to the Lord.

However, there were other potential avian candidates that peoples in other cultures historically have sacrificed such as chickens – birds found in Israel several centuries before the time of Jesus.

The first explicit biblical mention of doves dates back even earlier than Abram. In Genesis chapter 8 we read that Noah sent out a dove from the ark on three occasions. Twice it returned to the ark and on the second occasion came back with evidence of fresh plant growth, demonstrating that the floodwaters were receding. Noah sent out the dove again a week later, but this time it failed to return:

Then he sent out a dove to see if the water had receded from the surface of the ground. But the dove could find nowhere to perch because there was water over all the surface of the earth; so it returned to Noah in the ark. He reached out his hand and took the dove and brought it back to himself in the ark. He waited seven more days and again sent out the dove from the ark. When the dove returned to him in the evening, there in its beak was a freshly plucked olive leaf! Then Noah knew that the water had receded from the earth. He waited seven more days and sent the dove out again, but this time it did not return to him.

Why did Noah choose a dove for the task? Did he know about the bird's homing instinct, i.e. that it would probably return to the ark? And why did the dove fail to return that third time? It presumably entered the ark originally as one of a pair and Noah might have reasonably supposed it would return to its mate.

Let's turn to the Song of Songs where the dove terminology is used very differently, and perhaps surprisingly, in the context of sexual love. This short book contains six references to doves and half of these references use the word 'dove' as a term of endearment – a man describing his female lover affectionately as a dove:

… but my dove, my perfect one, is unique, the only daughter of her mother, the favourite of the one who bore her.

chapter 6 verse 9

It is interesting that both male and female lovers describe

the eyes of their beloved as being or being like doves. Each is physically attracted to the other and tenderly describes aspects of their lover's body with their eyes being singled out as objects of beauty.

His eyes are like doves by the water streams, washed in milk, mounted like jewels.

chapter 5 verse 12

Why did the author make such a link? We are not told how the lover's gaze could be compared with a dove. Does the mention of jewellery suggest the eyes sparkle? Does the talk of "water streams" suggest clear eyes? But why "washed in milk"? Or is this all simply a case of beauty being 'in the eye of the beholder'?

Only two other biblical references to doves associate the bird with love. Both of these are found in the Psalms and describe the nation of Israel affectionately as God's dove. The writer of Psalm 74 pleads to God in some despair not to allow his 'dove' to be destroyed by Israel's enemies. By contrast the writer of Psalm 68 declares gloatingly that "the wings of my dove are sheathed with silver, its feathers with shining gold", apparently in noting Israel's enrichment with silver and gold plundered from defeated Canaanite kings. However, the most well known reference to doves in the Psalter today comes from Psalm 55 and stems from its usage as the opening line of Mendelssohn's nineteenth-century hymn: "I said, 'Oh, that I had the wings of a dove! I would fly away and be at rest'."

The author was probably King David who wrote the psalm

as a prayer for God's help. Beset with fear and overwhelmed by horror, David wished he could simply fly away from trouble and employed the imagery of a dove's wings as a metaphor. Curious that he didn't think of an eagle's wings.

Five of the books of the Prophets contain a total of nine references to doves and all of these are shown below. Each reference makes some association with an aspect of the bird's natural attributes or behaviour. More mention is made of the 'moaning' of doves – a clear reference to their calls and song. Note how the prophet Ezekiel likened the repentant cries of people in Israel fleeing on a future day of God's judgement to the sound of doves, or how Nahum in pronouncing God's judgment on the Assyrian empire declared that their female slaves would beat their breasts and moan like 'doves'. All four references to the voice of doves seem to be negative with their talk of 'moaning'. What a contrast to the only other biblical reference to dove vocalisation back in the Song of Songs, where in chapter 2 the man commented favourably on the 'cooing of doves' as he wooed his female lover.

I cried like a swift or thrush, I moaned like a mourning dove.

Isaiah 38 verse 14

We all growl like bears; we moan mournfully like doves.

Isaiah 59 verse 11

Who are these that fly along like clouds, like doves to their nests?

Isaiah 60 verse 8

Even the stork in the sky knows her appointed seasons, and the dove, the swift and the thrush observe the time of their migration.

Jeremiah 8 verse 7

Abandon your towns and dwell among the rocks, you who live in Moab. Be like a dove that makes its nest at the mouth of a cave.

Jeremiah 48 verse 28

The fugitives who escape will flee to the mountains. Like doves of the valleys, they will all moan, each for their own sins.

Ezekiel 7 verse 16

Ephraim is like a dove, easily deceived and senseless - now calling to Egypt, now turning to Assyria. When they go, I will throw my net over them; I will pull them down like the birds in the sky. When I hear them flocking together, I will catch them.

Hosea 7 verses 11–12

They will come from Egypt, trembling like sparrows, from Assyria, fluttering like doves....

Hosea 11 verse 11

It is decreed that Nineveh be exiled and carried away. Her female slaves moan like doves and beat on their breasts.

Nahum 2 verse 7

Other aspects of dove behaviour are also noted in the Prophets. Jeremiah noted their migratory habits in chapter 8 and their breeding habitat in chapter 48. That comment about a dove nesting at a cave's mouth suggests a specific species of dove – caves and cliff faces are one of the habitats historically associated with Rock Doves and their feral pigeon 'kin'. There are also two references to the flight of doves. Hosea 11 talks about the 'fluttering of doves', an aspect of their flight as they take off or land. Isaiah 60 mentions unspecified creatures flying like clouds and comparing them to doves returning to their nests. This dove metaphor presumably suggests that these creatures were flying strongly and directly in straight lines, unlike say the undulating flight patterns of birds like the woodpecker. Perhaps the reputation of doves as strong fliers capable of flying considerable distances was already well known.

That curious reference in Hosea 7 is the most negative reference about doves and pigeons in the entire Bible. The prophet described a national enemy of Israel, the land of Ephraim, as being 'like a dove, easily deceived and senseless' as its leaders sought to forge alternating military alliances. But why the metaphor? What did the prophet mean by suggesting doves are stupid? The clue seems to come in verse 12 where the prophet claimed that doves could be easily lured and trapped. Was this something he did himself or had witnessed by watching hunters at work?

Let's turn to the New Testament. Again there are nine references in total to doves and pigeons, and all are found in the Gospels. The first of these chronologically is found in Luke chapter 2 verses 22-24:

When the time came for the purification rites required by the Law of Moses, Joseph and Mary took him to Jerusalem to present him to the Lord (as it is written in the Law of the Lord, "Every firstborn male is to be consecrated to the Lord"), and to offer a sacrifice in keeping with what is said in the Law of the Lord: "a pair of doves or two young pigeons."

Jesus was taken as an infant by his parents to the temple in Jerusalem to be presented and dedicated to God, and for his mother Mary to offer a sacrifice for her ritual purification after childbirth. His parents were too poor to afford a lamb and instead offered two birds as required by the Mosaic regulations specified in the book of Leviticus chapter 12. At the time Jesus would have been little more than forty days old and presumably would have no memory at all of this episode as an adult. Yet thirty years later when he entered the temple again and drove out the moneylenders, Jesus deliberately targeted the sort of people from whom his parents had purchased their two birds. Here's the account of Jesus cleansing the temple from John's Gospel in chapter 2:

In the temple courts he found people selling cattle, sheep and doves, and others sitting at tables exchanging money.... To those who sold doves he said, "Get these out of here! Stop turning my Father's house into a market!"

It seems that Jesus was particularly incensed by the actions of the dove sellers, but why? As a Jew fully conversant with the Law of Moses, he appreciated that in his day the regulations still required animals and birds to be sacrificed. Did he think that his parents in the past had been exploited when buying birds for sacrifice and he could still observe those practices of exploitation when he re-entered the temple?

The most well known set of biblical references about doves and pigeons relate to the baptism of Jesus. All four Gospels record this key event marking the start of Jesus's public ministry and all refer to the appearance of a dove. Here are the extracts from the Gospels of Luke and John:

When all the people were being baptized, Jesus was baptized too. And as he was praying, heaven was opened and the Holy Spirit descended on him in bodily form like a dove....

Luke 3 verses 21, 22a

Then John gave this testimony: "I saw the Spirit come down from heaven as a dove and remain on him."

John 1 verse 32

I am reluctant to offer a commentary when so much has been written about it over the centuries including much

41

speculation about that appearance of a dove and its symbolism. However, I will offer some views and questions to ponder. Firstly, the four texts together make clear that something that physically resembled a dove descended on Jesus as he came out of the river Jordan after his cousin John the Baptist had performed on him the 'baptism of repentance' rite. These do not describe how the dove descended on Jesus, but it is possible that the 'bird' fluttered down – the flight behavioural trait noted centuries earlier by Hosea.

Secondly, the only people who saw this dove about whom we are explicitly told were John the Baptist and Jesus himself. The writers of the three synoptic gospels tell us that Jesus saw the bird, but John's Gospel tells us that the Baptist saw it, testified to its appearance and claimed it to be divine, "coming down from heaven". Only Luke identifies this dove specifically as the Holy Spirit, although it seems appropriate to associate the other three gospel references to 'the Spirit' as being the Holy Spirit.

Thirdly, there is a key point about omission and what these texts do *not* say. There is no description of the dove's appearance in any reference – for example, nothing to suggest it had either white or any other particular colour of plumage. This is important to realise as virtually all pictorial depictions of the baptism show the dove being 'white' – a colour associated with purity and God's presence in the Jewish scriptures (see Psalm 51 verse 7 and Daniel 7 verse 9). Hence some commentators have argued that a white dove descended on Jesus both to symbolise his divine purity and to reinforce a message about God's presence at the baptism – a scene highlighting the

Trinitarian nature of God as Father, Son and Holy Spirit. However, these commentaries are based, probably mistakenly, on the perception that the dove was white. As I noted earlier in this chapter, doves come in various hues and colours, but the colour 'white' is not one of them. They can be bred in captivity to be 'white', but that is not their natural colour and there is no reason reading the translated texts to suppose this dove was white.

Let's expand this key point. The dove at the baptism of Jesus did not necessarily symbolise 'purity'. However, it clearly symbolised the presence of the Holy Spirit as the four Gospel writers stated. Why? We are so familiar with this story that it is easy to ignore some of the obvious questions these accounts pose on reflection. Why did the Holy Spirit appear in the bodily form of a dove? Why not, say, an eagle - a bird with various divine associations in the Old Testament as in Ezekiel 1? Nowhere else in the Bible does God the Spirit take this avian form? No doves descended at Pentecost, no mention of doves perching on Old Testament prophets like Elisha (who we read in 2 Kings chapter 2 received a double portion of God's Spirit), neither did Paul, Agabus nor any other Christians 'led by the Spirit' refer to doves. So why did Jesus and his prophetic cousin see a dove and what did they think it symbolised? We can only speculate, but it's at least a reasonable assumption to make that Jesus was very familiar with doves and pigeons. They would have been common, widespread and visible to anyone with observant eyes. Moreover, Jesus knew his Jewish scriptures and that the Law of Moses specified pigeon-doves to be the bird of sacrifice for the poor. We know that Jesus had visited the temple in Jerusalem when he was twelve years old (see Luke 2 verses 41-50) and it is likely he went thereafter with his parents annually. Over those two decades he would have seen many pigeon-doves being traded and sacrificed as sin offerings to symbolise repentance by the people who purchased them.

Imagine the scene. Jesus was marking the beginning of his public ministry by travelling some distance from Galilee to be baptised in the river Jordan, alongside crowds of other people. Did he already sense in some way that this emerging ministry would eventually require his life sacrifice as the ultimate sin offering? Did Jesus see a dove and perceive it as a sign of a divine ordained destiny that would take him to the Cross? Did Jesus also consider the harmless and vulnerable nature of pigeon-doves, birds so easily slaughtered by temple priests tasked with their killing? Did John the Baptist on seeing the dove also think of Jesus being sacrificed, alluding to that link the very next day when he saw Jesus again? He testified about Jesus on that occasion, saying in John 1 verse 29, "Look, the Lamb of God, who takes away the sin of the world!"

Our final Gospel reference takes up that point about vulnerability and I have left it until last, partly because of that theme. In Matthew 10 we read that Jesus sent out the twelve disciples with instructions to proclaim the 'kingdom of heaven'. The instructions he gave contained the following warning and advice for countering the hostility they would inevitably face:

I am sending you out like sheep among wolves. Therefore be as shrewd as snakes and as innocent as doves.

What did Jesus mean by that dual requirement? Why in particular did he tell his disciples to be like doves? Precisely what did Jesus mean about doves being "innocent"? It's interesting that English translations of this verse in Matthew use either the word "innocent" or "harmless" roughly in equal measure, which suggests that these two words are interchangeable in meaning one and the same thing. But are they? "Innocence" implies a state of blamelessness, of being without fault and therefore 'pure' in some way. Perhaps it suggests a certain naivety... of lacking guile. On the other hand, describing someone or something as being "harmless" simply says that it is not a threat. The description might imply it is ineffectual or even weak. Hence the choice of "innocent" or "harmless" might be the difference between Jesus commanding his apostles to "be pure" or to "be weak" - hardly one and the same! I think it is instructive that Jesus linked two imperatives inasmuch that he instructed his disciples to be both shrewd and innocent. Given the personal dangers they were going to face, it is readily understandable that he told them to be shrewd, preparing them to be cautious and on their guard. That suggests to me that the translation of the word as "harmless" is the more appropriate. Jesus was not instructing his disciples to be in any sense naive. He fully knew and prepared the twelve to expect trouble, persecution and even death. Yet his counter-cultural, 'upside down' kingdom message required his followers to confront hatred with love, to "turn the other cheek". As his followers today, we are charged with obeying that same instruction, to be harmless to those who show hostility to the Gospel message. Easy to say, but virtually impossible using our own strength. Perhaps we need the presence of a docile and vulnerable bird with us.

Questions To Consider

1. Why did Noah choose a pigeon-dove?

2. What do you think the dove symbolised at the baptism of Jesus?

3. Innocent or harmless? Which should we be as followers of Jesus today?

4. Which aspects of pigeon-doves teach you more about God?

The Eagle

Have you watched an eagle fly? It's a wonderful sight and causes me to marvel. I look in awe at the large bird with very long wings. It seems to own a patch of sky as it soars and slowly circles. Others before me have marvelled too. Three thousand years ago one of the writers of Proverbs expressed amazement at 'the way of an eagle in the sky'. The first-century Roman writer Pliny the Elder wrote in his book *Natural History* with admiration about sea-eagles diving on fish and their contests pursuing water birds. Shakespeare in his play *Cymbeline* described the "holy eagle" stooping in flight and the "royal bird prunes the immortal wing and cloys its beak, as when its god

47

is pleased".[5] Poets too have marvelled. The nineteenth-century British romantic poet Alfred Lord Tennyson watched eagles in the Pyrenees, from where he probably drew the inspiration for his brief poem, 'The Eagle'. It closes with the sentence, "He watches from his mountain walls, and like a thunderbolt he falls."[6] In his identically titled poem the twentieth-century American poet Edwin Curran waxed lyrically about the "Bird of the mighty wing", closing his piece with the line "Thou art like lightning driven flashing over paradise".[7] However, in recent years it's not only been writers who have marvelled and taken inspiration from eagles in flight. Think of groups as diverse as rock bands and sports teams choosing to name themselves after the bird. Here in Britain we remember an individual sportsman by his avian epithet. In the 1988 Winter Olympics the British ski jumper Michael Edwards became a household name as 'Eddie the Eagle', even if his exploits of 'flying through the air' didn't quite match this bird's prowess.

Eagles in Profile

Eagles are among the largest birds in the world and several species have wingspans measuring more than two metres in length. There are about sixty species across the world with the vast majority being found in Eurasia and Africa. They are daylight hunting birds which kill considerable varieties of animals - mammals, birds, reptiles, amphibians and even fish in the case of fish-eagles. Typically an eagle uses flight to hunt;

spotting potential prey while flying, swooping down, grabbing it and carrying it to a perch where it kills and eats its victim. Not surprisingly, eagles have keen eyesight with an ability to spot prey items from a considerable distance - a physical attribute due to their large eye pupils.

Their flight is another strength. Using their proportionately long wings eagles have the ability to fly fast, glide, soar, occasionally hover and even hang motionless facing a head wind. Some species migrate considerable distances between their breeding grounds and wintering areas. For example, Steppe Eagles today breed in central Asia and winter on the African savannah. As they migrate, many cross over southern Israel as I suspect their ancestors did during biblical times - a highly visible phenomenon of diurnal migration that people noted and is probably is one of the reasons why eagles feature so prominently in scripture.

Eagles are powerfully built birds with strong talons as feet to grip their prey and large, heavy hooked beaks designed for ripping the flesh from the animals they kill. They come predominantly in various shades of brown. Not all their plumages can be described as 'uniform' with their various mixes of dark, pale, rufous and even white colouring, but none can claim to be multi-coloured except perhaps the Bateleur with its striking combination of black, white and chestnut feathering. Females are typically larger than males. Both can live up to twenty-five years in the wild, but most die in their first five years before reaching maturity and a minority are killed early on in the nest by larger and older siblings. The nests themselves are known as 'eyries' and are built by both parents in tall trees or on rock ledges on mountains or coastal cliffs.

Vocalisation varies between different species of eagle, but none are known to 'sing' with complex melodies in the manner, say, of a warbler or a thrush. Instead, their typical voices are mixes of cries, whistles and barking sounds. It's interesting to note that some species like the Golden and Steppe Eagles are described in the *Collins Bird Guide* as being "rather silent" in contrast say to the "fairly vocal" Imperial Eagle. I will never forget my first encounter with the latter on a winter's day in central Spain as it barked and sounded just like a dog! As many as twelve species of eagle have been recorded in modern Israel. Only the Golden and Bonelli's Eagles are resident today, and two species formerly bred - the Greater Spotted and White-tailed Eagles. The full list also includes the Booted, Lesser Spotted, Steppe and Short-toed Eagles which all can be common on passage; the Eastern Imperial Eagle which is an uncommon winter visitor, and the Verreaux's Eagle which is an occasional visitor. The remaining duo on the list are rare or very rare, each with only a handful of recent records - the Tawny Eagle and the Bataleur.

Eagles in Folklore

Is the eagle the king of birds? Some might say no and argue in favour of a trickster wren, but there is little argument in terms of symbolism that the eagle has been the pre-eminent avian symbol of political power and authority across northern Eurasia and the Middle East. In ancient Greece eagles were identified with the god Zeus who according to one legend became an eagle in order to kidnap Ganymede of Troy. Ancient Romans associated eagles with Jupiter, the supreme god in their divine pantheon, and images of eagles were displayed as the battle standards of Roman army legions. It became practice to release an eagle over the funeral pyre of a Roman emperor in order for the bird to carry his soul heavenward. Little surprise thereafter for powerful and ambitious rulers like Charlemagne and Napoleon to adopt the eagle as a military symbol or political regimes like the Hapsburg, Russian and German empires as a national emblem.

Eagles have loomed large in myths and folklore across the world. In North America the legendary weather controlling 'thunderbird' recalled in the stories of indigenous peoples was probably based on the eagle.[8] Eagle feathers still feature prominently in the ceremonial clothing of native Americans, for example the headdresses worn by the Nez Perce peoples in Idaho. In Mexico the Aztecs followed a prophecy and centred their empire on a place where an eagle killed a snake. In south and east Asia eagles have been revered in Hindu, Buddhist and Jain traditions, largely because of their association with the legendary Garuda, the mortal enemy of snakes. This divine creature typically of human form with the wings and beak of an eagle is the national symbol of both Indonesia and Thailand, as well as the symbol of the Mongolian capital, Ulan Bator. The idea of being carried on eagles' wings resonates with people in the region because Garuda is identified in Hindu culture as the vehicle or vahana for the god Vishnu. Eagles also feature in Christian tradition and folklore as it has developed over the centuries in Europe. There are stories about individual saints and eagles, including a lovely tale about my local saint, the seventh-century Cuthbert of Northumbria, who was provided with a fish to eat by a White-tailed Eagle. By that time an eagle had became the symbol of St John, the gospel writer, and was depicted to represent him in the magnificent Lindisfarne Gospels. The ninth-century Irish theologian John Scotus Eriugena explained this link in his commentary on John's prologue. He argued that both the eagle and St John share the ability to see farther – the latter seeing deeper into the essence of God.

The most visible proof that eagles became part of European Christian folklore can still be seen in many churches. There are probably more images of eagles inside church buildings across Europe than of any other bird – even the dove. And the reason? The use of an eagle with outstretched wings as the design for the lectern – the reading stand which is used to rest a copy of the Bible. The tradition in Britain is several hundred years old and predates the Reformation.

My Encounters With Eagles

I have watched plenty of flying eagles. Here in Britain I have had several memorable encounters with Golden Eagles in flight including a jaw-dropping moment in Northumberland on a summer's day in the 1990s when two adult Golden Eagles flew close directly overhead. I have watched Booted Eagles in France circling far below me in a deep gorge, while in Portugal I have looked at the 'landing lights' on an adult bird's upper wings as it came closer and closer towards me. I have stared at various Short-toed Eagles hovering as they hunted for reptiles, but my best view was the surprise find of an autumn migrant Short-toed Eagle flying close and above my head as we walked along the Bocquer Valley in Mallorca. On one occasion in Germany I gasped in amazement at the sight of a huge White-tailed Eagle as the flying bird was the size of a barn door! And I have witnessed eagle migration over Israel. The impressive sight one March morning of a stream of single birds and small groups of Steppe Eagles flying northwards over Eilat en route to their distant breeding grounds has stayed with me as a memory and caused me to ponder those references to flying eagles in the Bible.

Eagles in The Bible

Eagles are mentioned in the Bible more than any other kind of bird except the dove. Nearly all the twenty eight eagle references are found in fifteen books across the Old Testament including all four of the major prophets. The final book of the New Testament also contains eagle references; a total of three including the last scriptural reference to any bird. Yet I find it surprising to realise that there are no eagle references in the

Gospels and that Jesus made no mention of them.

EXODUS	chapter 19 verse 4
LEVITICUS	chapter 11 verse 13
DEUTERONOMY	chapter 14 verse 12
	chapter 28 verse 49
	chapter 32 verse 11
2 SAMUEL	chapter 1 verse 23
JOB	chapter 9 verse 26
	chapter 39 verses 27–30
PSALM 103	verse 5
PROVERBS	chapter 23 verse 5
	chapter 30 verse 19
ISAIAH	chapter 40 verse 31
JEREMIAH	chapter 4 verse 13
	chapter 48 verse 40
	chapter 49 verse 16
	chapter 49 verse 22
LAMENTATIONS	chapter 4 verse 19

EZEKIEL	chapter 1 verse 10
	chapter 10 verse 14
	chapter 17 verses 3-7
DANIEL	chapter 4 verse 33
	chapter 7 verse 4
HOSEA	chapter 8 verse 1
OBADIAH	chapter 1 verse 4
HABAKKUK	chapter 1 verse 8
REVELATION	chapter 4 verse 7
	chapter 8 verse 13
	chapter 12 verse 14

The historical association of eagles as symbols of power and authority across cultures can be seen in the Bible. Indeed, we shall see that individual rulers like King Nebuchadnezzar of Babylon in scripture were described as eagles, as well as approving comments made about the physical power of eagles in flight. However, there are also biblical references to the tenderness and caring behaviour of parent eagles. In the Bible God is likened to an eagle as much for his loving protection as for his power. Several references in the Bible relate to various physical attributes of eagles, notably their speed in flight, and these seem relatively straightforward to understand. However, there are also curious and less understandable references to mysterious creatures appearing in prophetic visions that have the face of an eagle. Let's consider a representative selection of these eagle references in turn, beginning with God's words to Moses.

You yourselves have seen what I did to Egypt, and how I carried you on eagles' wings and brought you to myself.

Exodus 19 verse 4

These words were part of the first discourse between God and Moses on Mount Sinai in the early days of the exodus. Here God instructed the patriarch to remind the Israelites that their escape from Egypt was entirely due to his power and protective care. God likened his actions to that of an eagle carrying them on its wings to safety. It's a lovely image of a powerful protector removing the vulnerable from danger into his own safe and secure presence, and it's used as a recurrent metaphor with minor variations in several biblical references. However, it's also curious why an eagle is chosen. Did Moses and his contemporaries think that eagles carried their young to safety? Was it an observation? There is scant modern evidence that eagles or other birds of prey carry their young, but I have repeatedly seen water birds like the Great Crested Grebe with young chicks hunkered down on their backs as they swim. Note that in this reference God likens himself to a bird, albeit a very powerful one.

These are the birds you are to regard as unclean and not eat because they are unclean: the eagle....

Leviticus 11 verse 13

It is unsurprising that eagles were featured in the parallel lists of creatures in Leviticus and Deuteronomy which the Israelites were banned from eating. All creatures that kill or eat dead flesh were prohibited as part of a wider ban on eating animal blood. What is interesting is that the eagle was the very first creature to be listed (in both lists) and that only one type of eagle is mentioned, in contrast say to owls where six kinds were listed. Was there no awareness of the likelihood that several kinds of eagle could be found? I would speculate that people at that time did not differentiate between species like, say, the Golden and Steppe Eagles as these would appear very similar in terms of plumage, shape and size to people without modern optics.

In a desert land he found him, in a barren and howling waste. He shielded him and cared for him; he guarded him as the apple of his eye, like an eagle that stirs up its nest and hovers over its young, that spreads its wings to catch them and carries them aloft. The Lord alone led him; no foreign god was with him.

Deuteronomy 32 verses 10-12

Wonderful words about God's loving provision that were sung by Moses "in the hearing of the whole assembly of Israel" shortly before he died. He was reminding the Israelites that they had been chosen by God to be his people whom he would protect and care for. Again we have the image of an eagle which offers protection as it flies. Yet this image is much more developed. The bird is a parent watching over young nestlings, shielding and guarding them. It hovers over them protectively, carries them in flight and catches them on its wings when they fall, although the mention of it stirring up the nest is less than clear. Overall, this is a very tender image in which Moses compared God to a bird which demonstrated parental loving care.

Saul and Jonathan - in life they were loved and admired, and in death they were not parted. They were swifter than eagles, they were stronger than lions.

2 Samuel 1 verse 23

Words written by David who had heard the news that King Saul and his son Jonathan had been killed in battle and he composed a lament which he ordered the people of Judah to be taught. As part of his eulogy, he described the agility and strength of the two men being swifter than eagles - birds renowned for flying fast.

Does the eagle soar at your command and build its nest on high? It dwells on a cliff and stays there at night; a rocky crag is its stronghold. From there it looks for food; its eyes detect it from afar. Its young ones feast on blood, and where the slain are, there it is.

Job 39 verses 27-30

Part of a lengthy reply made by the Lord in response to Job's complaints. He reminded Job that the making of the earth, its weather and its inhabitant creatures all bear witness to the majesty, authority and justice of God who provides for all his creation. The Lord completed his first discourse with these closing words about the eagle – a farsighted predatory bird with the ability to soar in flight, build its nest at altitude and spot its prey from distance.

Praise the Lord, my soul, and forget not all his benefits.... who satisfies your desires with good things so that your youth is renewed like the eagle's.

Psalm 103 verses 2, 5

Even youths grow tired and weary, and young men stumble and fall; but those who hope in the Lord will renew their strength. They will soar on wings like eagles; they will run and not grow weary, they will walk and not be faint.

Isaiah 40 verses 30, 31

Let's take these two references together as they draw on a common theme, even though they were probably written three hundred years apart. David's psalm is the earlier. It speaks of God satisfying the psalmist's desires to such an extent that he feels youthful again, perhaps in a manner that proverbially matches an eagle's strength, but I find its meaning less than clear. There is an English idiom about feeling 'as strong as an ox' and this might have been an equivalent Jewish phrase circulating in King David's time.

By contrast, the connection between these words from Isaiah 40 and eagles is readily apparent. People who trust in God, whether young or old, will be spiritually strengthened. They will feel energised, feeling able to walk without fainting, run without tiring and fly high like an eagle. Obviously, the prophet was using metaphorical language, but these are words that still resonate today and which modern hymn writers incorporate. For example, the hymns 'Lord, I come to You' and 'On Eagles' wings' both contain lyrics about soaring like an eagle.

Cast but a glance at riches, and they are gone, for they will surely sprout wings and fly off to the sky like an eagle.

Proverbs 23 verse 5

There are three things that are too amazing for me, four that I do not understand: the way of an eagle in the sky, the way of a snake on a rock, the way of a ship on the high seas, and the way of a man with a young woman.

Proverbs 30 verses 18, 19

Here are two references to eagles in the wisdom literature of Proverbs. The first is unattributed as part of the thirty 'Sayings of the Wise', but the second is one of the sayings of Agur, described as "an inspired utterance"! The former reminded the reader not to trust in riches that can disappear in an instant (to put it in modern parlance), but I prefer this proverb's language about riches sprouting wings and flying away, presumably with the stealth of an eagle. As for Agur's saying, it reads as the words of someone marvelling at an eagle's flight - perhaps the way it can soar high and swoop down at speed.

This is what the Lord says: Look! An eagle is swooping down, spreading its wings over Moab.

Jeremiah 48 verse 40

Look! An eagle will soar and swoop down, spreading its wings over Bozrah. In that day the hearts of Edom's warriors will be like the heart of a woman in labour.

Jeremiah 49 verse 22

Both these references from Jeremiah were prophecies that were made six centuries before Christ about God's judgement falling on two of Israel's enemies – the nations of Edom and Moab. The prophet warned that judgement would be swift like a predatory eagle swooping down. Some biblical commentators have identified this 'eagle' to be the Babylonian king, Nebuchadnezzar. There would be a poetic irony if indeed it was as we shall see with the reference from Daniel chapter 4.

Their faces looked like this: Each of the four had the face of a human being, and on the right side each had the face of a lion, and on the left the face of an ox; each also had the face of an eagle.

Ezekiel 1 verse 10

Each of the cherubim had four faces: One face was that of a cherub, the second the face of a human being, the third the face of a lion, and the fourth the face of an eagle.

Ezekiel 10 verse 14

At the age of twenty nine the Jewish priest Ezekiel, living in Babylonian exile, saw a powerful vision of God's glory and it marked the start of his vocation as a prophet. At both the beginning and end of that vision Ezekiel saw four beings of human appearance, but each had four faces and four wings. As the vision progressed, it became apparent that these beings were creatures associated with God's heavenly presence - the cherubim (first mentioned in the Bible standing guard east of Eden back in Genesis 3). Mention in chapter 10 of the face of a cherub may seem confusing, but in that same chapter Ezekiel twice stated that these creatures he saw at the close of his vision were the same as the four he saw as it began. We should therefore deduce that the ox is being called a cherub - a starkly contrasting image to the chubby-faced children we associate with the cherubs of Baroque art!

Why the four faces and why was one the face of an eagle? The book of Ezekiel does not offer an explanation and we don't know even if the prophet sought one. Yet the strange imagery of these four-faced creatures has been a subsequent topic of voluminous commentary. Today there seems to be considerable agreement that the four faces are representative images of animal creation: the lion as the most powerful wild beast, the ox as the strongest domestic animal, the eagle as the mightiest of birds and the human as God's appointed ruling creature on the earth. It's interesting that all these creatures could fly, although no mention is made of soaring. Presumably the eagle's face was at the creature's back behind the human face, although Ezekiel did not make that explicit. Was that intentional and significant? Today we use a phrase about having 'eyes at the back of your head' in relation to situations where you need to watch closely what is going on around you. Could it be that far-sighted eagle eyes were needed for each visionary creature facing backwards? Perhaps it symbolised God's all-seeing nature?

Say to them, 'This is what the Sovereign Lord says: A great eagle with powerful wings, long feathers and full plumage of varied colours came to Lebanon. Taking hold of the top of a cedar, he broke off its topmost shoot and carried it away to a land of merchants, where he planted it in a city of traders. He took one of the seedlings of the land and put it in fertile soil. He planted it like a willow by abundant water, and it sprouted and became a low, spreading vine. Its branches turned toward him, but its roots remained under it. So it became a vine and produced branches and put out leafy boughs. But there was another great eagle with powerful wings and full plumage. The vine now sent out its roots toward him from the plot where it was planted and stretched out its branches to him for water.

Ezekiel 17 verses 3-7

By contrast, the other reference to eagles was explained by Ezekiel to his audience at the time. He told the Israelites an allegorical story about two "great eagles" and the bulk of that story is recounted above. Ezekiel's description of the first eagle breaking and carrying off part of a tree matches our knowledge today about eagle nest-building behaviour, but his mention of that bird's plumage being varied in colour is more curious, given the typically uniform appearance that eagles have. However, we don't need to speculate whether the prophet had a specific eagle in mind. Ezekiel clearly did, as he went on to explain in chapter 17. That eagle was none other than the mighty ruler of Babylon, King Nebuchadnezzar, who had captured Jerusalem and taken the king of Judah and many of its people including Ezekiel into exile. Those Jews remaining in Judah were represented in this allegory by the low-spreading vine. Initially that 'vine' was subject to Nebuchadnezzar, but Zedekiah the puppet king he set up in Judah reneged on his oath and turned towards the second eagle – identified by Ezekiel as Pharaoh, the ruler of Egypt. Such treachery by the king was a serious sin according to Ezekiel who predicted that the Egyptians would not intervene on Judah's behalf and that Zedekiah would be taken as a prisoner to Babylon and die in exile there.

Immediately what had been said about Nebuchadnezzar was fulfilled. He was driven away from people and ate grass like the ox. His body was drenched with the dew of heaven until his hair grew like the feathers of an eagle and his nails like the claws of a bird.

Daniel 4 verse 33

This eagle reference is all the more fascinating in the light of Ezekiel's allegory of the two eagles. Like Ezekiel, Daniel lived in Babylonian exile and was perhaps a contemporary, but there is no evidence that they knew of each other. Unlike Ezekiel, Daniel was known to Nebuchadnezzar and indeed became one of his top officials, thanks to his divine gift for interpreting dreams. One dream proved terrifying to interpret as it involved telling the Babylonian king of the temporary insanity he would experience until he acknowledged God's sovereignty over all kingdoms including his own. Verse 33 above summarized what happened as it came to pass. Recall that the prophet Ezekiel identified the king as a great "long-feathered" eagle in his allegory and consider how Nebuchadnezzar's hair grew so long to resemble eagle feathers and his nails grew more bird-like, perhaps like eagle talons.

Daniel said: In my vision at night I looked, and there before me were the four winds of heaven churning up the great sea. Four great beasts, each different from the others, came up out of the sea. The first was like a lion, and it had the wings of an eagle. I watched until its wings were torn off and it was lifted from the ground so that it stood on two feet like a human being, and the mind of a human was given to it.

Daniel 7 verses 2-4

Another dream in the book of Daniel, but one dreamt on this occasion by Daniel himself, during the first year of Belshazzar, Nebuchadnezzar's son, ruling Babylon. Daniel was told that each of the four beasts were sequential political empires and that the first of these was Babylon ... symbolised as a lion with the wings of an eagle. The second beast looked like a bear and the third beast as a leopard with four heads and four wings. We are told that the fourth beast was especially powerful with iron teeth and ten horns, and that Daniel in the dream was frightened by it and was "deeply troubled" by the dream's interpretation.

The first living creature was like a lion, the second was like an ox, the third had the face of a man, the fourth was like a flying eagle.

Revelation 4 verse 7

As I watched, I heard an eagle that was flying in midair call out in a loud voice: "Woe! Woe! Woe to the inhabitants of the earth, because of the trumpet blasts about to be sounded by the other three angels!"

Revelation 8 verse 13

The woman was given the two wings of a great eagle, so that she might fly to the place prepared for her in the wilderness, where she would be taken care of for a time, times and half a time, out of the serpent's reach.

Revelation 12 verse 14

The three eagle references shown above are the only ones found in the New Testament and they are confined to its last book - Revelation. The first from chapter 4 with its four living creatures should seem familiar as it echoes Ezekiel's inaugural vision. In his vision in Revelation chapter 4 the author John described how he looked into heaven and saw a divine figure on a throne surrounded by four living creatures. Each resembled an animal - the same four animals seen by Ezekiel - but in John's case each living creature had only the one face, six wings, eyes all over its body and was constantly praising God. In John's vision the creatures were evidently heavenly beings living in the presence of God. No explanation was given about their appearance and why for example one of these four resembled a flying eagle. However, the similarities with Ezekiel's creatures are so strong that we can presume John's four creatures were also representative of animal creation, with the eagle specifically representing avian creation. Hence it was seen and heard praising God on behalf of all the birds, just as the lion for all the wild beasts and the ox for all domestic animals.

As John's vision unfolded, he saw seven angels with seven trumpets and each sounded their trumpet in turn. The incident described in the chapter 8 eagle reference took place after the sounding of the fourth trumpet and the turning of sun, moon and stars to darkness by a third. While John was watching he heard an eagle in flight calling out loudly in a human language the word "Woe" three times for people on earth to hear and be warned. The fifth angel then sounded his trumpet and a plague of locusts descended.... I don't pretend to understand much of this imagery, but it is noteworthy that the eagle was heard with a loud human voice communicating directly with people. This reference is the only one in the Bible of any bird (not just an eagle) speaking in the human tongue, and in this case the eagle is warning human hearers of impending, divine judgement. The flying eagle was therefore acting as an agent on God's behalf – in this case prophetically as it warned people of the punishment about to come.

Let's turn to chapter 12 and the final eagle reference in the Bible. It makes a positive contrast to its immediate predecessor as it contains an allusion to God's loving protection. In the reference a woman (the mother of God's chosen ruler) was being pursued by Satan (the serpent), but she was given a pair of eagle wings so that she could fly to a place of safety. Hence the final eagle reference parallels the first back in Exodus in which God reminded the Israelites of his protective care, likening his actions to an eagle carrying them on its wings to safety. What a lovely image, both of God and of the bird typically selected to represent all birds.

Questions to Consider

1. How is your strength renewed like the eagle's?

2. Do you find the choice of eagle to symbolise God's loving parenthood powerful or curious?

3. Can you explain why Ezekiel's heavenly beings have the face of an eagle?

4. Is it significant the eagle is the sole bird in the Bible with a human voice?

The Chicken

Chickens are by far the commonest birds in the world. By 2016 their numbers had grown to more than 22,000 million and that total continues to rise.[9] Nearly all these birds are domestic and 'captive' as they are kept enclosed within factory style buildings. The vast majority live very short and sometimes painful lives before being killed for human consumption. These birds typically exist in the crowded and dim-lit conditions of intensive, industrial style 'broiler' units for only six to eight weeks before being slaughtered, plucked and prepared for people to buy as meat. The global scale of chicken farming today is huge and it continues to grow. People's food diets across the world are changing, particularly in Asia as a consequence of urbanisation and poverty reduction. The USA, China and Brazil as a trio of countries currently produce nearly half the world's chicken meat, estimated to be 116 million metric tonnes in 2016.[10] By my calculation that means more than 70,000,000 million birds are now being born and killed annually for meat.[11] In addition, hundreds of millions of female chickens are kept as 'layer hens' for egg production, producing over 1,350 million eggs in 2016.[12] These hens are typically kept alive little more than a year to lay up to three hundred eggs each before they too are killed and used as ingredients in processed foods like chicken soup. In his book *Birds and People* the British naturalist Mark Cocker describes these processes in further detail and he argues with good cause that the mistreatment they entail is one of the most glaring cases of systematic human cruelty towards another sentient animal.[13]

Chickens in Profile

There are hundreds of different varieties or 'breeds' of domestic chicken around the world today, but they all share a common ancestry in probably originating from one species of fowl. The Red Junglefowl is the wild ancestor of our domestic chickens and is native to southeastern Asia. It is one of many kinds of heavily built, ground-living birds of the family Phasianidae which also includes grouse, partridge, pheasants and turkeys. The male Red Junglefowl has brightly coloured plumage, for example its long golden-orange/deep-red crown and neck feathers and a metallic green tail, conspicuous red facial skin and throat, a red fleshy crest (known as a 'comb') and two red flaps of skin or 'lappets' hanging down either side of his face. The hen bird is more drab, having brown–gold plumage. Both sexes have powerful legs and strong feet that include a hind toe. The bird feeds by foraging on the ground for seeds and insects, making use of its feet to scratch away the surface. It flies low, does not sustain flight over any distance and is essentially sedentary. Its voice is distinctive. During the breeding season male birds announce their presence by making a loud and piercing cry – the well-known 'cock-a-doodle-doo' call or crowing.

The term 'breed' in this context is used to refer to a population of chickens that have been selectively bred to develop specific physical characteristics and behavioural traits that are passed on to their offspring. Here in the UK we have well over one hundred 'breeds' of chicken that are monitored and regulated by the British Poultry Club – the world's oldest extant organisation governing the rearing of chickens.[14] Various physical features are used to distinguish chicken 'breeds' including their size, feather plumage and skin colours, overall amount of feathering, variations of 'comb' and the colour of their eggs.

Providing a profile of chickens in modern Israel requires us to focus on farming. Chicken farming is big business in Israel today as elsewhere. A 2010 estimate suggested that Israeli people eat 1,700 million hen eggs and 430 thousand tonnes of chicken meat annually, which by my calculation amounts to 260 million birds.[15] Virtually all chicken farming is for the local market, but a small amount of chicken meat is exported to the USA to the Jewish-American kosher market.

Chickens in Folklore

There is a wealth of folklore, myth and custom associated with the chicken. It was probably the first bird to be domesticated, perhaps as early as eight thousand years ago in South-East Asia. We know roosters were kept in ancient Greece as cockfighting was mentioned in the play *The Birds* by Aristophanes, and that the Greeks also sacrificed roosters to seek medical advice from their god of medicine. The ancient Romans also sought advice by using chickens as they kept them for fortune telling, especially during times of war. Even today chickens are being sacrificed in some parts of the world. Their ritual killing is part of Santeria and other voodoo religious practices in parts of West Africa, Brazil and the Caribbean. In Israel ultra-orthodox Jews still kill chickens during the festival of Yom Kippur as part of their 'kaparot' ritual, explicitly declaring that the birds are being sacrificed as a rite of penitence on their behalf, despite promotional campaigning by the Ministry of Agriculture encouraging people to use an alternative such as giving money to the poor.[16]

Cockfighting has been a 'sport' for millennia and is allegedly the world's oldest sport still in existence. It involves two or more male birds with sharp metal spurs attached to their hind legs being released into a small encircled arena known as a cockpit in order that they fight, sometimes to the death. It was practiced in ancient Greece and Rome, and spread throughout the latter's empire, perhaps even to Britain. It became part and parcel of English culture for much of the last millenium with kings like Henry VIII and James I being keen patrons, before it was outlawed in 1849. Yet the practice still flourishes today elsewhere in the world, especially among Hispanic communities in Mexico, Central America and the Philippines where it is regarded as a national sport. However unpleasant it may seem to many of us, others argue with some justification that the existence across rich industrial countries of factory farms in which chickens are kept indoors, intensively reared and killed within eight weeks for their meat is the more cruel. Either way, chickens are made to suffer.

In traditional Japanese culture, male chickens are revered as the birds which greet the dawn. There is an ancient tale about the sun goddess being lured out of a cave by roosters to dispel the darkness. Hence roosters are still kept at some Shinto shrines and have special perches provided in their honour next to the temple entrance. In Chinese culture the rooster continues to have great symbolic importance as the only bird featured in the zodiac. It is the tenth sign and every tenth year in a twelve-year cycle is designated as the 'Year of the Rooster' - the last such year being 2017. People born in the rooster year are allegedly more honest, intelligent, independent and good at communication, but they also have tendencies to be impatient, critical and selfish. Many millions of people follow the Chinese zodiac and allow it to influence both their personal and business decision-making.

Male chickens became an important Christian symbol and still feature on church buildings to this day. The sixth-century pope Gregory I claimed the rooster to be a suitable symbol of Christianity because of its association with St Peter. Three centuries later another pope Leo IV allegedly ordered that a rooster image should adorn the exterior of St Peter's Basilica in Rome and his successor Nicolas I subsequently decreed that one should be placed on every church steeple. Despite this historic papal association, many Protestant churches across Europe and North America also feature roosters typically as weathervanes at their highest point: for example, Dome Lutheran Cathedral in Riga, Latvia; St George's Tron church in Glasgow, Scotland, and the UCC church in West Barnstaple, Massachusetts, USA.

Let's return to food. Chickens are *the* birds we eat in increasing numbers across the globe, especially with the changes in diet and food culture as a consequence of globalisation. While the fast food chain McDonalds takes the flak as the most visible indicator of cultural homogenisation, we should also remember the influence of Kentucky Fried Chicken in exporting fast food culture, especially to China where it remains the largest restaurant chain at the time of writing in 2018. Here in Britain, where so-called 'ethnic' foods are now staple to our diet, a prominent politician in 2001 famously pronounced chicken tikka masala to be a national dish.[17] But why chicken? Is it the bland taste and uniform texture? Is it more adaptive or malleable for flavouring? Do people choose it on health grounds as a low cholesterol alternative to our traditional red meats? Or is it simply a matter of price for being comparatively cheap to buy?

Mark Cocker in his book surveys many more of the folk tales, customs and cultural associations people have with chickens in different parts of the world. He argues how they demonstrate our affinity as an animal species with a bird claimed to be "a human with feathers" - a bird of symbolic importance across so many religions and cultures.[18] Cocker notes the chicken has historically been such a precious possession providing us with vital food, and yet we continue and readily choose to abuse it and sacrifice it as a scapegoat for our human failings.

My Encounters With Chickens

My encounters with chickens are typical of most people in rich industrialised countries. I rarely see live birds, but each week I eat chicken eggs and meat. My favourite foods include several that are chicken-based; boiled eggs for breakfast, egg mayonnaise sandwiches, chicken stews, curries like chicken Balti and roast chicken itself. Christmas dinner in our household usually consists of a large roasted chicken with all the trimmings, as we don't much like roast turkey. As I said, my encounters are typical of many. Chicken for me is a food commodity that I buy in packaged form at the supermarket. No feathers, no skin, no blood, no indication of avian life! By contrast, Sheila, my wife, had the personal experience of growing up with live chickens. As a very young girl she had a pet hen that she named 'Marian' after her favourite aunt. The bird was like a friend to her and she recalls playing with the hen, including her attempts to push it to and fro on the garden swing. Of course, the sad day came when the hen met her demise and ended up on a plate being served for dinner, having been swiftly despatched by Sheila's mum who had wrung the bird's neck.

While I rarely see chickens, I have heard them frequently in the past. I live in a village where a few people on occasion have kept hens and the occasional rooster. I can well recall hearing the male birds making those loud and shrill crowing sounds, during the day and even in the early hours towards the dawn. It's clearly an avian family trait. At the time of writing, the loudest local bird sounds include the pheasants and Red-legged Partridge in the fields behind our house as they cry, call and 'chunter' - particularly at dusk.

Chickens in The Bible

The word 'chicken' does not appear in most translations of the Bible. Instead, three words are used in my bible, the New International Version, to denote this one kind of bird; the American term 'rooster' for the male bird, the 'hen' for the female and one usage of 'poultry' to signify chicken meat. Yet I have grouped the fourteen biblical references despite the different terminology used to describe them. Adding these references together, the chicken becomes the third most cited kind of bird in the Bible. Unusually, most of these avian references are found in the New Testament with eleven references in the four gospels.

Each day one ox, six choice sheep and some poultry were prepared for me, and every ten days an abundant supply of wine of all kinds. In spite of all this, I never demanded the food allotted to the governor, because the demands were heavy on these people.

Nehemiah, 5 verse 18

After returning from Babylonian exile Nehemiah was appointed as governor of Judah and focused on rebuilding the defensive wall around its capital, Jerusalem. Unlike his predecessors, Nehemiah did not take advantage of his power by taxing people, but he fed one hundred and fifty people daily with meat that included poultry. Hence we have here a record of people in southern Israel at around 430BC eating meat that was probably chicken.

There are three things that are stately in their stride, four that move with stately bearing: a lion, mighty among beasts, who retreats before nothing; a strutting rooster, a he-goat, and a king secure against revolt.

Proverbs 30 verses 29-31

The Old Testament book of Proverbs offers many observations about nature and these include some of the Sayings of Agur found in chapter 30. This comment about the "stately bearing" of a rooster as he struts around his territory reads as a positive and perhaps surprising interpretation of its behaviour, comparing the bird to a human king or to the "king of the beasts".

Although we don't know much about Agur himself, it seems reasonable to suppose his proverbs dated from around the same time as the rest of the book of Proverbs which was primarily written during King Solomon's reign nine centuries before Christ. If that was the case, we can deduce that roosters were known to people in Israel nearly three thousand years ago.

Who gives the ibis wisdom or gives the rooster understanding?

Job 38 verse 36

Another extract from the Lord's speech to Job found in chapters 38-41. It reads as a lengthy series of questions for Job to consider, all of which testified to God's sovereignty and power. The Lord began with talk of inanimate creation – the earth, sea, sun, weather and the stars – before mentioning animals and birds. The rooster was the second living creature to be mentioned. The accompanying footnote in the NIV Bible states that both the ibis and the rooster were birds "whose habits were observed by people to forecast the weather". Quite how is not made clear, but this comment makes sense in explaining why the verse is found midway through a discourse on the weather.

Therefore keep watch because you do not know when the owner of the house will come back - whether in the evening, or at midnight, or when the rooster crows, or at dawn.

Mark 13 verse 35

Jesus warned his followers with these words to watch and be ready for his Second Coming. He told them that only God the Father knows when that time will be, and he used a parable about a man going away and leaving his servants in charge of his house. The owner could return at any time during the night as he explained, even when the rooster crows well before the dawn. In those days the occupying Roman troops had a change of guard at 3am – the start of the fourth watch. This was sounded by a bugle known as 'the cockcrow', presumably because people noted roosters began crowing around that hour in anticipation of the new day.[19] Hence Jesus was warning that the owner of the house could return at any hour, even those times of night when people would expect to sleep.

"Truly I tell you," Jesus answered, "this very night, before the rooster crows, you will disown me three times."

Matthew 26 verse 34

Then he began to call down curses, and he swore to them, "I don't know the man!" Immediately a rooster crowed. Then Peter remembered the word Jesus had spoken: "Before the rooster crows, you will disown me three times." And he went outside and wept bitterly.

Matthew 26 verses 74,75

"Truly I tell you," Jesus answered, "today - yes, tonight - before the rooster crows twice you yourself will disown me three times."

Mark 14 verse 30

Immediately the rooster crowed the second time. Then Peter remembered the word Jesus had spoken to him: "Before the rooster crows twice you will disown me three times." And he broke down and wept.

Mark 14 verse 72

Jesus answered, "I tell you, Peter, before the rooster crows today, you will deny three times that you know me."

Luke 22 verse 34

Peter replied, "Man, I don't know what you're talking about!" Just as he was speaking, the rooster crowed. The Lord turned and looked straight at Peter. Then Peter remembered the word the Lord had spoken to him: "Before the rooster crows today, you will disown me three times." And he went outside and wept bitterly.

Luke 22 verses 60-62

Then Jesus answered , "Will you really lay down your life for me? Very truly I tell you, before the rooster crows, you will disown me three times!"

John 13 verse 38

Again Peter denied it, and at that moment a rooster began to crow.

John 18 verse 27

Eight references from the four gospels, but all related to one distressing episode in the final hours before the crucifixion. During the last supper Jesus told the twelve disciples that they would all desert him that night which Peter vehemently denied. In response Jesus predicted that Peter would thrice deny knowing him. After the arrest of Jesus later that night, the clarion call of a rooster's crow would act as an immediate and bitter reminder to Peter of his denial. We are told nothing about the bird, other than he crowed twice, presumably in quick succession. However, we are told by John in his gospel chapter 21 how Jesus in a resurrection appearance reinstated Peter in front of the other apostles by pointedly asking him three times if he loved him. Is this a model of forgiveness that the sight of a rooster can remind us about?

"Jerusalem, Jerusalem, you who kill the prophets and stone those sent to you, how often I have longed to gather your children together, as a hen gathers her chicks under her wings, and you were not willing."

Luke 13 verse 34 & Matthew 23 verse 37

These are some of the most poignant words that Jesus said. They form a lament about the future of Jerusalem, the most holy city for Jewish people who were required to worship God in the great temple that was built there. Jesus prophesied the city's destruction as an act of divine judgement and he expressed his sorrow at that prospect – a devastating event which took place forty years later when Roman troops destroyed the city.

Jesus in these words likened himself to a female bird. He described wanting to be like a mother hen protecting her chicks under her wings. Tragically, unlike those chicks Jerusalem was unwilling to turn to him and seek his loving protection. Despite its grim context, I find this image very reassuring in its tenderness. Jesus wanted to protect the people of Jerusalem like a hen with her wings outspread over her baby young. A picture of 'God with us', not as an Almighty figure, but as a tender and caring mother bird.

The idea of God's motherhood was developed further by the medieval Christian mystic, Julian of Norwich. In *Revelations of Divine Love*, her account of sixteen visions she experienced during one day in 1373, Julian wrote about the trinity of God as Father, Mother and Lord. As well as describing Jesus as our brother and saviour, she described him as our mother as well. Julian wrote, "So we see that Jesus is the true Mother of our nature, for he made us. He is our Mother, too, by grace, because he took our created nature upon himself. All the lovely deeds and tender services that beloved motherhood implies are appropriate to the Second Person."[20]

Questions to Consider

1. Should Christians feel uncomfortable about intensive methods of chicken farming?

2. Is the rooster a suitable symbol of Christianity?

3. How should we 'keep watch' in the words of Mark 13?

4. Does it help you to consider the motherhood of God?

The Owl

Owls are the favourite birds of many people in Britain today. I know from my experience as a wildlife guide in North-East England that owls provide their 'wow' moments when people are watching birds. Many of my customers have told me that the sight of a Short-eared Owl hunting in daylight among the sand dunes was the memory they treasured after a day out with me on Holy Island. Watching the bird flying slow and low, back and forth, as it hunts for voles and other prey. Seeing its large and enigmatic yellow eyes that seem to stare at you. For others the Barn Owl is their favourite. A ghostly white apparition at dusk hovering above the field margin - always mysterious and a special encounter. Consider as well the popular images of owls in our contemporary culture: 'Owl' advising Winnie the Pooh in the Disney films; the seafaring companion of a pussycat in Edward Lear's nonsense poem, and Hedwig and the postal owls at Hogwarts School in the Harry Potter books. Think too of the soft toys you might buy today for children to cuddle. It's not only teddy bears, but also cuddly owls online including miniature Snowy Owls like the sort we bought our young daughter.

Owls in Profile

Across the globe there are up to two hundred and fifty species of owl belonging to the *Strigiformes* order. They are found in every continent except Antarctica and in most habitats - forest, Arctic tundra, alpine mountain, farmland, tropical jungle and desert. Two-thirds are in the southern hemisphere. Generally they are meat-eating predators that hunt at night, although a large proportion are crepuscular in that they hunt both at dawn and dusk. They range hugely in size and weight. The European Eagle Owl is one of the world's heaviest raptors and can weigh up to 4.6kg - in contrast to the sparrow-sized Elf Owl of the American southwest that weighs only 40g. Their plumages for both sexes are generally similar and tend to be brown, grey and cream in tone with variations in patterns of barring, streaking and spotting.

Despite their considerable variation in size, owls are instantly recognisable due to three distinctive features. They have big heads, round faces and large forward-facing eyes. Those eyes are proportionately among the largest for any animal including us, enabling them to see in the very low light intensity of night. They cannot turn their eyes which are locked by bone into their sockets, but they can instead turn their heads by as much as 270 degrees to see objects around and behind them. Their round faces comprise facial discs which typically form concave saucers surrounding each eye and these operate somewhat like satellite dishes in capturing and directing sound to the ears.

The hearing ability of owls is even more impressive than their eyesight. Ears are generally large vertical openings on either side of the facial disc that are hidden from view by feathering. They are positioned asymmetrically with one higher than the other, enabling the owl to pinpoint the direction of a sound with exceptional accuracy. It's been calculated that the hearing of a Barn Owl is at least ten times more powerful than human hearing.[21]

Owls do not build nests. Most nest in tree cavities or in rock crevices, and many will take over the old nests of other birds like crows and other raptors. The females take the major share of nest duties including incubation and brooding, but both sexes share feeding duties for their young which typically remain at the nest site for several weeks after hatching.

Voice is the one aspect of owl behaviour above all else featured in mythologies around the world. As predominantly nocturnal creatures, owls are much more heard than seen and the sounds they make are often disliked. Their calls are mixes of screeches, hoots, moans, hisses, croaks and whistles - sounding unmusical and even eerie to the human ear. Unsurprisingly, owl vocalisation does not typically feature among people's favourite birdsong.

Modern Israel is home to seven resident species of owl, a further three either are seen in winter or on passage and one species is now extinct – the Brown Fish Owl last recorded in 1975. Both Barn Owls and Little Owls today are common throughout the country, in contrast to the Pharaoh Eagle Owl which has rarity status as a resident in the desert areas. The full list of owls recorded on the national checklist for the modern era is as follows: Barn Owl, Tawny Owl, Hume's Owl, Eurasian Eagle Owl, Pharaoh Eagle Owl, Brown Fish Owl (recently extinct), Long-eared Owl, Short-eared Owl, Little Owl, Eurasian Scops Owl, Pallid Scops Owl.

It's tempting to compare this list with the six kinds of owl recorded in the Old Testament books of Leviticus and Deuteronomy from three thousand years ago. Tempting, but probably unwise! One bird on that latter list seems readily identifiable – 'the white owl'. Surely this is the Barn Owl which is currently common in the region. The only other white owl found anywhere today is the Snowy Owl of the Arctic tundra; unsurprisingly, it's never been recorded in the area. I would also speculate that 'the great owl' from the Old Testament list was likely to have been the Eurasian Eagle Owl – by far the largest owl on Israel's modern list. However, the references to the 'horned owl' and 'little owl' on that list present dilemmas. Could there be three possibilities for 'horned owl' on the modern list? Both species of Eagle Owl as well as the Long-eared Owl have prominent ear tufts that appear like horns.

Nor should we assume that the Mosaic references to 'little owl' can be readily identified as the Little Owl today. There are two other candidates which are smaller in size – either of the two species of Scops Owl.

Owls in Folklore

No other kind of bird has experienced such a change in terms of human popularity. Owls today are loved by people, but it was not always so. Owls have been feared and despised across the world throughout the ages. The ancient Romans considered owls as birds of ill omen – associated with doom and death. Native American cultures like the Aztecs and the Maya viewed them as symbols of death and destruction, and the Apache peoples warned that someone would die whenever an owl was heard hooting. Yet others by contrast have venerated owls. The ancient Greeks worshipped Athena, the goddess of war and wisdom; her consort was an owl, hence owls were consequently revered in Athens. In India owls have been associated with the Hindu goddess Lakshmi and therefore held sacred, but they have also been feared as messengers of death. In Japan the Ainu people on Haikkaido island historically revere the local fish owl as "the god who protects the village".[22] More widely, in modern Japanese culture many people wear owl (fukuro) charms to bring them good luck and protect against hardship.

Even today owls are feared as bad omens in some communities

across the world who associate the various calls of owls with sorcery and misfortune. As recently as April 2012 a Jamaican blogger was imploring her readers not to throw stones at owls because of superstition.[23] Use of owls in black magic has allegedly been a key factor in the illicit owl trade in India according to a 2010 report.[24] Field research between 2000 and 2012 by Bruce Marcot revealed that rural people he met across southern, central and east Africa continued to link owls with witchcraft and try to ward them off.[25] Yet attitudes towards owls in some parts of rural Africa are slowly changing to be more positive. A BBC report from Kenya in 2006 featured local man Paul Murithi running an owl sanctuary near Mount Kenya despite opposition in his village.[26] And at the time of writing in 2018 Naivasha Owl Centre in Kenya runs an educational programme with rural schools to counteract traditional hostility towards owls.[27]

My Encounters With Owls

Owls are among my favourite birds too. I have seen all five British breeding species within ten miles from my house and am fortunate to record both Tawny and Barn Owl on my garden list. Indeed, I share my study with a stuffed bird of each species – both were 'road kills' which sadly is a common fate for owls in the UK today. My British owl list also includes a vagrant Scops Owl found at Sunderland in September 2017 – coincidentally during my last week working for the local university. Yet my favourite memory is of a young Long-eared Owl which seemed curious to see me as I later recalled in a blog:

On 5 August 2003 I was walking in a local conifer wood when I saw a dark shape in the distance. It was a owl and it flew down the forest drive towards me. To my surprise it kept coming until eventually it flew over my head where it turned in a 90 degree arc and landed on the nearest tree - a four metre high Sitka spruce on my right. The owl looked intently at me for about half a minute before it took off, flew across the drive and landed on my left on another spruce, this time at head height. Again the bird looked at me, but this time it moved its head in a circular fashion as I have seen young Barn Owls do. After twenty seconds of this, it flew off and glided away down the track until it disappeared from view. Throughout the entire time it remained silent.

When I first saw the bird silhouetted in flight I had presumed it to be a Tawny Owl. However, when it landed I could see it had orange eyes and long flattened ear tufts. Add to that its 'flat wing' posture, the lack of a pale trailing edge to those wings and its relatively small size (clearly smaller than a Tawny Owl), and I knew I was looking at a young Long-eared Owl.

Why did the owl behave as it did? I don't wish to ascribe human motivation, yet I suspect that this bird was simply curious and wanted to take a closer look. Perhaps this young owl had never seen a human being before. Could that be the reason it was not alarmed enough either to make a cry or to raise those distinctive ear tufts? [28]

My most unusual 'owl' encounter was with a bird guide in Africa who imitated a local owl to startling effect. In November 2006 I was with friends on a birdwatching holiday in the Gambia where we hired a local guide. It was our first morning with Mas, we were walking through open bush and he began to whistle. Not just whistle, but a series of whistles that grew in volume and rose in pitch. Almost at once, various small birds hopped into view and they were clearly agitated. Mas was imitating the calls of the Pearl-Spotted Owlet and these birds came flocking to find it. The owlet is a rapacious hunter that eats prey items ranging from beetles to birds, but it is small as a 'pygmy owl' and therefore can be driven away by other small birds if they flock together and chase it off. We employed a couple of guides on that trip and each had the ability to make various avian calls in order to lure birds into view. Yet it was that first initial experience of Mas calling as an owlet that I most remember.

Owls in The Bible

All eleven owl references are found in the Old Testament. They feature in eight books, mainly in the prophetic writings with Isaiah alone having four references. Unlike our contemporary positive feelings towards owls, none of these references suggest that people in ancient Israel viewed the birds with affection. On the contrary, it seems that people were fearful of owls and what they signified.

These are the birds you are to regard as unclean and not eat because they are unclean: .... the horned owl, the screech owl.... the little owl... the great owl, the white owl, the desert owl....

Leviticus 11 verse 13, 16-18

You may eat any clean bird. But these you may not eat: .... the horned owl, the screech owl.... the little owl, the great owl, the white owl, the desert owl....

Deuteronomy 14 verse 11, 12,15-17

Once again we should consider these two parallel passages together – a summary in Deuteronomy chapter 14 and the full list of 'clean' and 'unclean' creatures in Leviticus chapter 11. This comprehensive list and the rules that applied to it were given by God in order for the Israelites to demonstrate their obedience to Him. As we have already discussed, the list of prohibited foods was lengthy. Not only did it include all birds like ravens that ate carrion, but also other meat-eating birds like the eagle, falcon and the owl.

What is also interesting in these two passages is the large number of owls listed with six different 'species' mentioned. No other family of birds is separated out and identified with such a number of species, even though we know today for example that there are even more kinds of eagle than owl in the region. Two owls are identified in terms of their size (great and little owls), two in terms of appearance (horned and white owls), one in terms of habitat (desert owl) and one on account of a sound it makes (screech owl). Whether or not these are identifiable as birds found in the region today, we should recognise that a mix of four qualitatively different criteria were evidently used to separate and distinguish between them. Presumably people were familiar with seeing at least four of these owls, perhaps a fifth (i.e. the desert owl), but not necessarily with seeing the screech owl – identified on the basis of its piercing call. Only three of these owls are featured elsewhere in scripture; there are no further references to horned, little or white owls. Five of these references speak of owls generically, but the psalmist, Isaiah in chapter 34 and the prophet Zephaniah all specifically mention the desert owl. The latter two also mention the screech owl which they apparently link with desert owls. Isaiah in chapter 34 is alone in mentioning the great owl which he links with the raven as a bird breeding in the desolation of Edom.

Compare these lists in the NIV translation with their counterparts in other translations like the New Revised Standard Version and the Jerusalem Bibles, and you will see considerable variation among the kinds of owls listed. The NIV lists six kinds of owl in these two passages, but the NSRV and Jerusalem each list only three. Yet the trios listed are completely different. The NRSV identically lists the little owl, great owl and desert owl for the eleventh, thirteenth and fifteenth bird types in common with the NIV in its translation of the Leviticus list of 'unclean birds', whereas the Jerusalem Bible has the screech owl for the eighth (in common with the NIV), but it has the horned owl for the eleventh and barn owl for the thirteenth. That choice of the barn owl for the thirteenth bird type instead of the great owl means that these three bible translations between them list seven kinds of owl, emphasising my earlier point about the surprisingly large number of owl kinds being mentioned.

I have become a brother of jackals, a companion of owls.

Job 30 verse 29

Job's claim was part of a lengthy, personal lament. Earlier in the same chapter he accused God of attacking him despite his pleas for mercy: "I cry out to you, God, but you do not answer; I stand up, but you merely look at me. You turn on me ruthlessly; with the might of your hand you attack me. You snatch me up and drive me before the wind; you toss me about in the storm. I know you will bring me down to death, to the place appointed for all the living." (Chapter 30 verses 20-23). Job lamented his physical suffering and social humiliation, sensing that he had become an outcast whom others detested and avoided. He perceived the only 'friends' left for him were wild dogs and owls.

I am like a desert owl, like an owl among the ruins. I lie awake; I have become like a bird alone on a roof.

Psalm 102 verses 6, 7

This cry is quite similar to the words from Job that we have just read. The psalmist prayed to God to hear him, but sensed that God was not listening. He was physically weak, abused by people who taunted him and he groaned in his distress.

The psalmist likened himself to a solitary owl, living like an outcast in an uninhabitable place. In the early verses he painted a picture of isolation and alienation, yet he continued the psalm with words of praise and a declaration of hope in God's unchanging nature. But what of the owl? Did the psalmist presume desert owls to be solitary? Was that a phenomenon he had observed?

But desert creatures will lie there, jackals will fill her houses; there the owls will dwell, and there the wild goats will leap about.

Isaiah 13 verse 21

I will turn her into a place for owls and into swampland; I will sweep her with the broom of destruction, declares the Lord Almighty.

Isaiah 14 verse 23

The desert owl and screech owl will possess it; the great owl and the raven will nest there. God will stretch out over Edom the measuring line of chaos and the plumb line of desolation.... She will become a haunt for jackals, a home for owls.... The owl will nest there and lay eggs, she will hatch them, and care for her young under the shadow of her wings....

Isaiah 34 verses 11,13,15

The wild animals honour me, the jackals and the owls, because I provide water in the wilderness and streams in the wasteland....

Isaiah 43 verse 20

Isaiah contains four references to owls and the first three

of these are remarkably similar. Each of these are words of judgement, prophesying destruction on different national enemies of Israel. In chapters 13 and 14 the target of the prophet's wrath was Babylon which he predicted would be overthrown and made uninhabitable. The once great city would be deserted by people. Only desert creatures like wild dogs and owls would live among the ruins of its palaces, fortifications and houses. The very name of Babylon would be wiped out and the city reduced to "a place for owls and into swampland". It's unclear to me if the prophet was making a clear link between owls and swampland as a habitat, but at least one type of owl that favours marshland (the Brown Fish Owl) is associated with the area in modern Iraq where Babylon was sited.

In chapter 34 it was the turn of Edom. The prophet declared that there would be great slaughter and destruction comparable to the overthrow of Sodom and Gomorrah. Edom would be made desolate and deserted. Its only inhabitants would be birds like the raven, falcon and three kinds of owl; desert animals like the jackal, hyena and goat; and plants like the nettle, bramble and thorn. Note in verse 15 that the unspecified owl would nest there, lay eggs, hatch them and care for her young "under the shadow of her wings" - a surprisingly tender and positive image in the context of such destruction.

That positive tone is echoed by the prophet in chapter 43 with a lovely verse referring to God's loving provision even for animals and birds that people despised. The prophet noted that God provided water for these desert creatures at the same time as He gave drink to Israel as His chosen people. Israel however did not express gratitude, unlike the owls and jackals which honour God. Here God loves even the unlovely creatures like owls and they in turn honour Him.

So desert creatures and hyenas will live there, and there the owl will dwell. It will never again be inhabited or lived in from generation to generation.

Jeremiah 50 verse 39

These words from the prophet Jeremiah are part of a long message about Babylon, prophesying its eventual destruction. It is similar in content to Isaiah's prophecy in predicting destruction with the city becoming uninhabitable and left to wild animals and owls to live in.

Because of this I will weep and wail; I will go about barefoot and naked. I will howl like a jackal and moan like an owl.

Micah 1 verse 8

We read in the first chapter of Micah that the prophet received a vision concerning Samaria's destruction that upset him deeply, causing him to shed his clothes and to weep and wail. With hindsight we know the Assyrian empire under its king Sennarcherib was to be the agent of that destruction in 720BC. Yet Micah's vocal grieving as he howled like a jackal and moaned like an owl was as much about the coming invasion of Judah which came to pass twenty years later.

Flocks and herds will lie down there, creatures of every kind. The desert owl and the screech owl will roost on her columns. Their hooting will echo through the windows, rubble will fill the doorways, the beams of cedar will be exposed.

Zephaniah 2 verse 14

By contrast to Micah, the prophet Zephaniah foresaw the destruction of Assyria itself as an act of God's judgement . He lived a century later than Micah in the seventh century before Christ, and his mention of owls is the last of the biblical references to them. Like the earlier prophecies of Isaiah, he claimed that owls would be among the creatures living in the kingdom's deserted ruins. Like the prophecy of Isaiah 34, he asserted that two kinds of owl would live there – both the desert owl and the screech owl.

Questions to Consider

1. Why do you think owls are so popular today?

2. What could owls symbolize about God's judgement?

3. Do you relate to the psalmist's self description as a solitary owl?

4. Can we learn from owls honouring God?

The Raven

Do a word association exercise. Think 'Gothic horror', then think 'bird' and close your eyes. What image comes into your head? The chances are that you see a big crow, even a raven ... the biggest, blackest and 'meanest' of all the crows. A symbol of doom and death. But is it really a villain or a victim? Perhaps no other bird has been so vilified in European mythology and suffered so much human persecution as a consequence. Here in Britain today our relationship with ravens is more complicated. As elsewhere in Europe, we slaughtered them with the shotgun by the tens of thousands in the nineteenth century and made them extinct across much of England. Yet we now as a nation pay someone specifically to look after a tiny number of pinioned birds in central London. The post of 'Raven Master' at the Tower of London was created in 1968 and the present incumbent has seven birds in his care - all named and ever popular with tourists.

Ravens in Profile

Ravens are the largest kind of crow and indeed are the largest of all perching birds or 'passerines' in Europe and Asia. They belong to the family Corvidae which today are highly successful with one hundred and fifteen species across the world including many that are increasing in range and population despite significant human persecution over centuries across much of their distribution. Ravens are found across the northern hemisphere in virtually every type of habitat apart from high density urban areas. They can be found in hot deserts like Israel's Dead Sea region as well as high altitude mountain terrain like the Himalayas. They are also adaptable in what they can eat - a diet described as ranging 'from a worm to a whale'.[29] They can eat vegetable matter, but they are adept at catching and eating live prey such as rabbits, rats and moles as well as a wide range of small and medium sized birds. But above all they are eaters of carrion, finding animal carcasses and picking them clean. Historically this has included human remains from battlefields and the gallows. In Britain there is evidence of prehistoric burial sites with exposed areas where bodies would be left for ravens and other crows to scavenge and pick over before the human skeletons were then removed and placed in covered burial chambers.

Ravens are bigger than Buzzards. They have been described as 'uber crows' – being as much as one third larger than Carrion Crows which they most resemble. Indeed, they make a strong claim to be the archetype crow: glossy black plumage; a huge, deep beak; flat shaped head; shaggy throat feathering; long deep body; long wings; powerful legs and feet, and a wedge-shaped tail. Ravens are superb fliers that are able to soar very high, glide and dive at speed. Their flight can appear playful with rolls and tumble dives, particularly when they perform their display flying. They are monogamous and pair for life, they are non-migratory and will sometimes remain in their territories all year, although these can cover large areas. Their voice is distinctive – low-pitched, loud and sounds like 'cronk'. In the breeding season their vocal repertoire can comprise a wide range of various clucking, knocking and grating sounds.

Measuring bird intelligence is a highly contentious issue, but many avian scientists claim that the corvid family of birds are clever and quick to learn. Ravens for example have the ability to cache food, especially in the breeding season, and to remember where they have stored it. One remarkable aspect of corvid activity seems to confirm the current view about their intelligence; their social behaviour demonstrating reciprocity through giving gifts, not only to each other but also to people. In her book, 'The Genius of Birds', US writer Jenny Ackerman records some amazing tales of 'gift giving' by various crows across America. She recounts the recent story of Gabi, a young girl in Seattle who began feeding crows on her way to and from the local bus stop. Gabi started on a daily basis later to leave peanuts out on a tray in her garden for the crows. She noticed from time to time that various artefacts would appear on the tray; an earring, screws, bolts, buttons, a tiny plastic tube, a rotting crab claw, a small scrap of metal printed with the word 'best', and even an opalescent white heart. It seemed that the crows were leaving these items in return for Gabi who has collected a selection over the years in plastic bags recording the dates when she found them.[30]

Today in Israel there are now three species of ravens found as breeding residents as well as six other corvids, some of which could be mistaken for different types of raven. The largest of these is the Raven (Corvus corax) itself, distinguished in size from the much commoner Fan-tailed and Brown-necked Ravens which otherwise appear very similar. In addition, Jackdaws and Hooded Crows are common breeders and Rooks overwinter. Indian House Crows also live in southern Israel today, but it is very unlikely they did so during the biblical era as they are much more recent arrivals, perhaps being a colonial introduction of the nineteenth century. Both Red-billed and Yellow-billed Chough are rare visitors today, but the Jay is a common resident in northern and central Israel. Given its variegated plumage with splashes of bright blue, however, I think it highly unlikely to be confused with 'any kind of raven'.

Ravens in Folklore

Ravens loom large in ancient and more modern mythologies across Europe, Asia and North America. Often they have been seen as birds of ill omen linked to death, for example as the ghosts of murdered people in Swedish folklore and damned souls in some German stories. In the Viking myths of northern Europe the Norse god of war and death, Odin, had two pet ravens, Hugin (meaning 'thought') and Munin ('memory'), that would perch on each shoulder. At the end of their daily flying missions they would report back to him what they had seen, enabling Odin to have omniscience and earning him the name of Rafnagud the Raven God. Vikings apparently believed that ravens can see long distance and therefore occasionally used them as maritime navigational aids. Out at sea a bird would be released from a boat and carefully watched as it flew up high. If it saw land, it would fly towards it, pursued below by the sailing crew who set their course to follow the bird. However, if the raven saw no land it would fly back to the boat.

The ancient Greeks associated ravens as messengers of the god Apollo who sent a white one to spy on his lover. On hearing the news of her unfaithfulness, Apollo scorched the raven in his fury, turning all its feathers black and ravens have ever since been black in colour. In native American myths (held for example by the indigenous peoples of the Pacific Northwest coast) the raven was viewed by some as the Creator of the world, by others as a cunning trickster and as being both in a myth told among the Haida peoples living along the Canada/Alaska border. According to their story, a raven freed some timid and scared creatures that were trapped inside a shell. These were the first men on the earth. The raven then found some women that were also trapped, freed them and then watched as the men and women coupled sexually. It seems similar tales were shared among indigenous peoples of the Russian Far East, indicating a history of cultural contact between peoples of the two continents. Further south in Japan and China, the raven was depicted in various myths as a three legged bird associated with the sun and was sometimes shown being coloured red.

Religious cultures in south Asia also feature ravens and crows. For example, the Hindu god Shani is depicted riding a giant raven. The national bird of Buddhist Bhutan is the raven which represents one of the main deities, Jarog Dongchen. At one time the raven was protected by 'pain of death' as it was a capital crime to kill one, and to this day ravens can be found nesting among Bhutanese monasteries and temples.

Ravens appear repeatedly in stories about various Christian saints. The fourth-century hermit, Paul of Thebes, living in a desert cave was provided with daily bread to eat by a raven who visited him for sixty years. St Benedict in the sixth century was protected on one occasion by a raven who removed poisoned food at the saint's request. Yet my favourite is a tale much closer to home and one I find to be more credible as it accords with 'gift giving' behaviour. It's a tale about St. Cuthbert, the seventh-century Northumbrian who had a remarkable affinity with local wildlife including birds, and it's recalled in *Cuthbert and the Animals* - a delightful compilation of tales about the saint retold by John McManners.[31] He noted how Cuthbert in later life moved from Lindisfarne to the Farne Islands with a desire to live as a solitary and spend more time in prayer. Nevertheless, monks regularly came from the mainland to visit Cuthbert so he built a guest house for his visitors. However, one day Cuthbert saw two ravens dismantling the thatched roof of that shelter, tearing off pieces of straw to use for nesting material. The saint told the birds "in the name of Christ" to leave the island and they flew away. Three days later one of the birds returned and came close to Cuthbert, lowered its head and behaved with recognizable contrition. The saint realised the raven was sorry, forgave it and told the bird that the two of them could return to the island. Thus pardoned, the bird flew off and fetched its mate. When they returned, both birds each carried a piece of hardened pig's lard which they dropped at Cuthbert's feet as gifts. Harmony was thus restored. The ravens stayed on the island for many years and Cuthbert became very friendly with them. He enjoyed explaining to visitors how these birds illustrated God's desire to forgive, restoring those who show by their actions that they are truly penitent. As for the pig fat, it was used in the guest house by visiting monks to grease their footwear.

My Encounters With Ravens

On 16 October 2013 I was working in my study when I heard a vaguely familiar bird call. "Sounds like a raven" I thought and looked out the window. I watched in amazement and growing excitement as I recognized the bird flying over our garden was indeed a solitary raven. It was flying only ten metres or so above the ground in a southerly direction and it was calling – that distinctive low-pitched 'cronk'. "Great. A new bird for the garden list", the nerd in the anorak whispered in my head. But what was a raven doing here? My sighting illustrated a change in local fortune for a bird so heavily persecuted in the past. In Northumberland, as elsewhere in northern Britain, raven numbers are increasing and birds are returning to lowland and coastal areas from which they disappeared a century ago.

I recognised the call that October day as I am quite familiar with ravens. Over the past thirty years I have seen and heard plenty across the British uplands. I think it's good news that their numbers are growing in the county where I live and I now expect to see ravens whenever I go walking in the Cheviot Hills. I love their deep, guttural calls. To my ear these sounds don't seem at all harsh, unlike the screams of a fellow corvid like the Jay, but rather soft and pleasing with their rolled 'r'. I like to see ravens in flight – their sheer size, long wings, protruding necks and diamond-shaped tails. Above all, it's what they do when they fly. Soaring, tumbling and rolling as they drop. Wow!

Ravens in The Bible

After forty days Noah opened a window he had made in the ark and sent out a raven, and it kept flying back and forth until the water had dried up from the earth.

Genesis 8 verses 6,7

The raven is the first identifiable kind of bird in the Bible. It was the first of two types of birds released by Noah, well after the flood waters had receded and the ark had come to rest. The tops of mountains were already visible, but Noah waited a further forty days before sending out a raven. Presumably it climbed up high in order to see into the far distance. It developed its own flying circuit across the sky as it flew backwards and forwards looking for land. We are not told for how long it flew this circuit, but at some unspecified point the raven disappeared and it seems Noah interpreted its disappearance as marking the moment when the floodwaters had dried up. Noah then released a dove "to see if the water had receded from the surface of the earth", but there is no mention how much time elapsed between the raven's disappearance and sending out the dove.

Over the centuries there has been plenty of conjecture and speculation proffered about the raven. Much of it has been negative, in essence claiming that the raven failed in its task and let Noah down because it did not return to the ark. The holy man therefore was compelled to release a dove which in due course would return to the ark with evidence of new growth. Some have argued that ravens have been despised by people ever since as a consequence.

Did the raven fail? The Genesis text offers no comment and we are compelled to surmise. Let's begin with the obvious question why Noah chose the raven in the first place. Perhaps we can presume Noah's avian knowledge was enhanced by living in close quarters with a 'floating zoo' and that he might have learned three key facts about the raven – its strong flight, its ability to see far and its carrion diet. Hence it made sense for Noah to choose a bird that could ascend and see long distances from a considerable height. He might also calculate that the bird would keep on flying until it could spot carrion on dry land to which it could fly down in safety and eat. Of course there would have been plenty of edible carrion floating on the surface of the flood waters, but a raven could not land on the water without the high risk of being unable to take off again.

The raven's disappearance was significant to Noah who knew it marked an important change in the level of receding floodwater. Yet he waited before sending out the dove. We don't know for how long he waited and it doesn't seem to have been long enough as the dove returned on the first occasion empty-beaked. But what of the raven? Did it do the job Noah expected of it?

These are the birds you are to regard as unclean and not eat because they are unclean: .... any kind of raven....

Leviticus 11 verses 13,15

You may eat any clean bird. But these you may not eat: .... any kind of raven.

Deuteronomy 14 verses 11,12,14

Let's consider these two parallel passages together. Deuteronomy chapter 14 contains a summary and Leviticus chapter 11 a full list of the creatures that the Israelites were either permitted or prohibited from eating. This list and the rules which applied to it was given by God in order for the Israelites to demonstrate their obedience to Him. Restricting the foods they ate in this way was a means of consecrating themselves as they sought to be holy in following the God who had rescued them from slavery in Egypt. God instructed them through Moses and Aaron as we read in Leviticus 11 verses 43 and 44: "Do not defile yourselves by any of these creatures. Do not make yourselves unclean by means of them or be made unclean by them. I am the Lord your God; consecrate yourselves and be holy, because I am holy." The list of prohibited foods was lengthy and included all birds like ravens that ate carrion. Today we now know that some creatures prohibited for consumption by these regulations might be unhealthy for people to eat, but it is not possible to distinguish between 'clean' and 'unclean' purely on the basis of health considerations. Whatever the reasoning for specific creatures being deemed 'unclean', these dietary restrictions became deeply embedded and defining elements of Jewish culture. Little wonder that Peter fifteen hundred years later was so appalled at being told to "kill and eat" unclean creatures including unspecified birds during a vision (see Acts 10 verses 9-23).

Note that each list in both books refers to "any kind of raven", probably in recognition of more than one species of raven in the region. However, these were not differentiated in these texts or elsewhere in the Bible.

Then the word of the Lord came to Elijah: "Leave here, turn eastward and hide in the Kerith Ravine, east of the Jordan. You will drink from the brook, and I have directed the ravens to supply you with food there."…. The ravens brought him bread and meat in the morning and bread and meat in the evening, and he drank from the brook.

1 Kings 17 verses 2-4, 6

This tale about the prophet Elijah features ravens in a unique role – the only account in the Bible where birds, or any other creatures, feed someone. Picture the scene. The northern kingdom of Israel was being ruled by a king, Ahab, who actively promoted worship of the pagan god Baal. In the words of 1 Kings 16 verse 33 Ahab "did more to arouse the anger of the Lord, the God of Israel, than did all the kings of Israel before him". A new prophet, Elijah the Tishbite, entered the stage and publicly opposed Ahab, prophesying an imminent and severe drought sent as a sign of God's displeasure and judgement on the evil king and his realm. Elijah was told to flee the kingdom and live 'beyond the Jordan' where he would be miraculously sustained – perhaps paralleling the situation faced by the Jews during the years in the wilderness when they were led by the great prophet Moses. Elijah went as instructed and stayed in the Kerith Ravine where he had water to drink from the brook and food provided by local ravens. They brought him

111

bread and meat twice each day to eat – a full diet that only a king at that time would expect to eat.

The text does not detail the identity of the meat, although we might presume it to be carrion and therefore 'unclean' according to the Law of Moses – a case perhaps of laws being superseded as and when an extreme situation required. Nor are we told for how long this situation persisted. Can we presume that ravens were chosen for this task because of their high intelligence? Or was this more about their behavioural trait of food storing which Elijah observed and took advantage of? What is clear from the scripture is that birds deemed 'unclean' according to Jewish law and generally despised by people were daily feeding God's prophet who was living in Gentile territory outside the promised land. What an honour for a crow!

Who provides food for the raven when its young cry out to God and wander about for lack of food?

Job 38 verse 41

He provides food for the cattle and for the young ravens when they call.

Psalms 147 verse 9

Let's take these two texts together as they each make the same point. God provides food for young ravens. Both verses echo the consistent assertion throughout the Bible that God's provision is plentiful for all of creation, including 'unclean' birds like ravens. Indeed, one of the names of God is Jehovah Jireh – the God who provides. As we shall see later, it's a point Jesus repeatedly made to his followers and used the example of ravens to illustrate.

The eye that mocks a father, that scorns an aged mother, will be pecked out by the ravens of the valley, will be eaten by the vultures.

Proverbs 30 verse 17

Another of the diverse range of tasks carried out by ravens! This chilling verse identifies ravens as agents of God's judgement, punishing people who disobey the fifth Commandment given to Moses on Mount Sinai: "Honour your father and your mother, so that you may live long in the land the Lord your God is giving you" (See Exodus 20 verse 12). Is this an example of bird behaviour being identified as having symbolic meaning? Ravens (and indeed other birds) can attack sick animals by pecking their eyes and thereby blinding them. It's a behavioural trait that has brought them into conflict with shepherds and goatherds over the centuries.

His head is purest gold; his hair is wavy and black as a raven.

Song of Songs 5 verse 11

By contrast, the Song of Songs makes reference to one of the raven's natural attributes as an aspect of beauty – its black colour. The female describes her male lover's body, commenting on different parts in turn beginning with his head and its wavy black hair. The phrase 'raven-haired' has subsequently passed into our language as a term usually associated with human beauty.

The desert owl and screech owl will possess it; the great owl and the raven will nest there. God will stretch out over Edom the measuring line of chaos and the plumb line of desolation.

Isaiah 34 verse 11

The final Old Testament reference is one of several prophecies in the book of Isaiah that link birds symbolically with God's judgement – in this case three kinds of owl and the raven. Unlike the proverb noted above, the raven is not so much enacting judgement, but instead demonstrating the passing of divine punishment on the nation of Edom simply by its presence. Again this is a case of the writer noting an aspect of bird behaviour and discerning symbolic meaning. Presumably the author of Isaiah 34 knew that ravens bred in uninhabited desert and wilderness areas, and was warning the people of Edom that their land would be made desolate and uninhabitable as a result of God's judgement.

Consider the ravens: They do not sow or reap, they have no storeroom or barn; yet God feeds them. And how much more valuable you are than birds!

Luke 12 verse 24

There is only one New Testament reference to ravens

and it's one of the teachings of Jesus himself. He echoed the singular point made centuries earlier in both the book of Job and the Psalms that God feeds ravens. As such, ravens should be considered as illustrations of God's generous provision and a reminder for us as people to get our priorities in order. Chapter 12 in Luke's gospel recounts the parable Jesus told of the greedy rich fool who focused on building up his already considerable wealth instead of thinking longer term about his life and his relationship with God. In Luke's account Jesus immediately followed up that story with teaching to his disciples telling them not to worry about their material needs. For "life is more than food, and the body more than clothes". In contrast to the greedy rich fool, ravens do not build barns to store their food, yet thanks to God's loving care they have plenty of food to eat and we should draw an obvious lesson from the fact of that divine provision.

This is hence the third biblical reference making the point that God's food provision for ravens offers a lesson about God's loving care for people. It's a lesson for us just as much today as when Jesus taught it. If birds don't need to worry about their material needs, then neither do we as God loves us even more than birds.

It is interesting to note that three of the ten raven references make this simple point about God's provision even for an 'unclean' bird like the raven. And, as we have seen, a fourth biblical reference inverts this point with the account of ravens at God's instruction miraculously feeding his prophet. Consider the ravens indeed and the various God-given tasks to which they have been assigned in the Bible.

Questions to Consider

1. Did the raven let Noah down?

2. What should we learn from Elijah and the ravens?

3. How does 'eye pecking' symbolise God's judgement?

4. Do you find it helpful to 'consider the raven'?

The Supporting Cast

There are a further eighteen kinds of bird specifically featured in the Bible and twelve of these have multiple references. Together they make up a diverse spectrum of birds that vary hugely in terms of their respective size and behaviour. Each is discussed in this chapter in the order of their frequency in scripture, beginning with the vulture which has a total of seven references. That makes it the sixth-most featured kind of bird in the Bible.

The Vulture

Two types of vulture appear in the parallel lists of foods prohibited for consumption - "the vulture" and the "black vulture" (Leviticus 11 verse 13 & Deuteronomy 14 verse 12). There are a further three Old Testament references to vultures, as well as two from the Gospels. Those latter references make it one of only five kinds of bird specifically mentioned by Jesus.

He wanders about for food like a vulture....

Job 15 verse 23

Words spoken by Eliphaz as part of a diatribe against wicked men. He claimed that their fate included the experience of hunger, compelling them to look for food "like a vulture".

The eye that mocks a father, that scorns an aged mother, will be pecked out by the ravens of the valley, will be eaten by the vultures.

Proverbs 30 verse 17

A proverb served as a warning - to obey the fifth commandment. In this context vultures act as God's co-agents of judgement through eating the bodies of people attacked by ravens as punishment for mistreating their parents.

Shave your head in mourning for the children in whom you delight; make yourself as bald as the vulture, for they will go from you into exile.

Micah 1 verse 16

Warning words from the prophet Micah that the people of Judah would go into exile. It came to pass in 586BC when they were taken captive by the Babylonians. The comment about vultures being bald refers to their lack of head feathering, giving them the appearance of baldness.

For as lightning that comes from the east is visible even in the west, so will be the coming of the Son of Man. Wherever there is a carcass, there the vultures will gather.

Matthew 24 verses 27, 28

"Where, Lord?" they asked. He replied, "Where there is a dead body, there the vultures will gather."

Luke 17 verse 37

Two references from two synoptic gospels, probably to the same words of Jesus. In Matthew's account these words about vultures gathering form part of a long discourse by Jesus about "the End Times" and the signs of its coming. He warned his disciples that false messiahs and prophets would appear and perform unspecified 'signs and wonders', but they should not be deceived. The actual coming of the Christ ("the Son of Man" in the words of Jesus) would be obvious with clear signs of his presence, paralleling the natural example of vultures being present around carrion meat. In effect Jesus was telling his followers to read the signs. Jesus drew attention to a natural phenomenon to use as a parable and he continued in the same speech to highlight the fig tree, again as a natural sign of imminent change.

The Stork

The stork also appears in the two lists of 'unclean' food that the Israelites were instructed not to eat. In both it was listed as the third from last bird identified (Leviticus 11 verse 19 & Deuteronomy 14 verse 18).

Such inclusion in these lists is unsurprising if you consider a stork's undiscriminating diet – I have watched plenty of storks in France and Spain eating garbage at rubbish tips.

The wings of the ostrich flap joyfully, though they cannot compare with the wings and feathers of the stork.

Job 39 verse 13

The trees of the Lord are well watered, the cedars of Lebanon that he planted. There the birds make their nests; the stork has its home in the junipers....

Psalm 104 verses 16, 17

Even the stork in the sky knows her appointed seasons, and the dove, the swift and the thrush observe the time of their migration. But my people do not know the requirements of the Lord.

Jeremiah 8 verse 7

Then I looked up – and there before me were two women, with the wind in their wings! They had wings like those of a stork, and they lifted up the basket between heaven and earth.

Zechariah 5 verse 9

Let's consider these four references as pairs. Both the psalm and the Jeremiah reference mention behavioural aspects of the stork. Overall, the psalm reads as a hymn that praises God for creation including the natural wonders of the earth. The lands north of Israel are extolled for their trees, animals and birds which include the tree-nesting storks. Jeremiah by contrast was lamenting the behaviour of the Israelites in failing to repent – not knowing what they should do, unlike the four specified kinds of birds that act when they should in migrating at the right times.

The Job reference is part of God's reply, testifying to his sovereignty and loving care of animate creation. Here it relates to the ostrich which we discuss later in the chapter, but let's note in this passage how the stork is contrasted as a bird with long feathers and wings enabling it to fly strongly. That aerial strength is implied in the strange reference from Zechariah. The prophet had a series of night visions including a seventh of a woman in a basket that an angel told him symbolised people's wickedness. In the vision two other women with the wings of storks lifted the basket up high and carried it off to 'Babylonia'. Most biblical references to birds with strong flight relate to eagles and this choice of the stork is unexplained.

The Quail

That evening quail came and covered the camp, and in the morning there was a layer of dew around the camp.

Exodus 16 verse 13

Now a wind went out from the Lord and drove quail in from the sea. It scattered them up to two cubits deep all around the camp, as far as a day's walk in any direction. All that day and night and all the next day the people went out and gathered quail. No one gathered less than ten homers. Then they spread them out all around the camp.

Numbers 11 verses 31, 32

He let loose the east wind from the heavens and by his power made the south wind blow. He rained meat on them like dust, birds like sand on the seashore. He made them come down inside their camp, all around their tents.

Psalm 78 verses 26-8

They asked, and he brought them quail; he fed them well with the bread of heaven.

Psalm 105 verse 40

All these references refer to an event during the exodus. Under the leadership of Moses, the Israelites had fled from Egypt into Sinai and embarked on a long trek eastwards through wilderness and desert towards the land promised to their ancestors Abraham, Isaac and Jacob. It was to prove very long, not such much in distance but in the forty years it took eventually for them to cross the Jordan river and enter Canaan. Within a few days of starting their trek people began complaining about the diet: "If only we had meat to eat!" (see Numbers 11 verse 4). In response God was angered and told Moses that he would provide enough meat to eat to last a whole month - to the point when people would loathe it. Then the wind blew, huge numbers of quail arrived from the sea and for two days people went out and gathered quail in abundance.

This event was clearly interpreted as a miracle, at least in retrospect by the psalmists who viewed it as an example of God's loving provision. Perhaps it was. However, the sudden appearance of migrating birds in large numbers is a frequently observed natural phenomenon. As birdwatchers we talk about 'falls' of migrants when an area can be blanketed with birds that have been blown off their normal course by strong winds. It's a phenomenon I have witnessed on several occasions during autumn along the Northumbrian coast when the winds are easterly, particularly when it's been raining and exhausted birds 'fall' from the sky and drop into whatever cover they can find - trees, bushes, even long grass. I have seen something similar in southern Israel with quail back in 1999. At the time I was birdwatching at Eilat - the seaside town at the northern end of the Gulf of Aquaba. It was early morning on 15 March in a local park and for an hour I watched in excitement as I saw a host of migrant birds stopping and feeding including several Quail. I wrote in my notebook at the time that I saw twenty new species that day (Red-throated Pipit, Olivaceous Warbler, Pallid Swift and Quail among them), but it was the sight of those quail in such apposite context that has stayed in my memory.

The Falcon

Only the list of 'unclean' birds in Deuteronomy mentions the falcon (Deuteronomy 14 verse 13). It does not appear in Leviticus and is indeed the only kind of bird featured in one list but not the other. Again the reference is to "any kind of falcon" in apparent recognition that that there were several species of falcon in the region. In modern Israel eleven species of falcon have been recorded including three which are resident - the Common Kestrel, Barbary and Lanner Falcons.

No bird of prey knows that hidden path, no falcon's eye has seen it.

Job 28 verse 7

These words come from an unattributed interlude to be found before Job's final defence. The writer speaks of precious stones and metals coming from hidden places deep below the earth's surface unknown to birds or beasts. People have tunnelled down and found these places, but they have not found wisdom. Only God knows where to find it. The falcon is specifically mentioned in this reference as part of a wider family of birds (the birds of prey), presumably because of its reputation for keen eyesight. The writer seems to be saying "even the falcon hasn't seen the hidden path".

...there also the falcons will gather, each with its mate.

Isaiah 34 verse 15

The third reference to falcons comes at the end of a prophecy against Edom, with the prophet declaring that it would be destroyed as a result of the Lord's 'day of vengeance'. In its ruins pairs of falcons would gather, alongside owls, ravens and various desert animals.

The Hawk

The two lists of foods prohibited for consumption mention "any kind of hawk", but no specific type of hawk is detailed (Leviticus 11 verse 16 & Deuteronomy 14 verse 15). In modern Israel five species have been recorded, but none are resident and only the Levant Sparrowhawk has common status as a passage migrant.

"Does the hawk take flight by your wisdom and spread its wings toward the south?...."

Job 39 verse 26

A question that God poses to Job during the first of his two replies to the complainant. It's interesting to note the comment about the hawk flying south - the direction today which hawks head in the autumn as they migrate towards their African wintering grounds.

The Ostrich

The wings of the ostrich flap joyfully, though they cannot compare with the wings and feathers of the stork. She lays her eggs on the ground and lets them warm in the sand, unmindful that a foot may crush them, that some wild animal may trample them. She treats her young harshly, as if they were not hers; she cares not that her labour was in vain, for God did not endow her with wisdom or give her a share of good sense. Yet when she spreads her feathers to run, she laughs at horse and rider.

Job 39 verses 13-18

Even jackals offer their breasts to nurse their young, but my people have become heartless like ostriches in the desert.

Lamentations 4 verse 3

Why was the female ostrich viewed as heartless? Was this a commonly held perception? Both these Old Testament references assert that this huge and flightless bird to be uncaring towards her young. However, in the first reference the Lord in his reply to Job balances criticism of the ostrich's limitations in parental behaviour with marvelling commendation about her ability to run fast and outpace people on horseback. The overall message is that even the ostrich bears testimony to God's sovereignty and loving care of creation. By contrast, the reference from Lamentations presents the ostrich in an entirely negative manner... as a metaphor. According to the anonymous prophet the Israelites had become heartless and cruel even to their own children during the invasion by Babylon.

The Swallow

Even the sparrow has found a home, and the swallow a nest for herself, where she may have her young - a place near your altar, Lord Almighty, my King and my God.

Psalm 84 verse 3

Like a fluttering sparrow or a darting swallow, an undeserved curse does not come to rest.

Proverbs 26 verse 2

There are only two biblical references to swallows and these also contrast sharply. The psalm delightfully expresses how God's temple is a sanctuary even for small birds whom the psalmist envies on account of their nearness to his altar. It reads as a beautiful prayer of longing by an author who yearns to be close in God's presence like the swallow with her young. The very next Old Testament book also contains one reference to the swallow, again in conjunction with the sparrow, yet its subject matter seems apparently much darker in tone. It's contained in a proverb that related to cursing - a hostile practice even today in some cultures that can induce considerable fear for those who have been cursed. These wise words from King Solomon imply that innocent people need not fear harm from curses as they won't take effect. They are likened to a swallow in fast flight mode darting here and there, apparently never coming to rest.

The Partridge

Now do not let my blood fall to the ground far from the presence of the Lord. The king of Israel has come out to look for a flea - as one hunts a partridge in the mountains.

1 Samuel 26 verse 20

Words from the fugitive David when he captured King Saul (who had been pursuing him) and spared his life. David described his king's actions as foolish as searching for a flea. It was an action David compared to hunting a partridge in the mountains - presumably a metaphor used then to describe futile activity as the bird was too hard to find there.

Like a partridge that hatches eggs it did not lay are those who gain riches by unjust means. When their lives are half gone, their riches will desert them, and in the end they will prove to be fools.

Jeremiah 17 verse 11

A proverb from the prophet Jeremiah whose meaning is clear even today. It's presumably based on a commonplace observation that some hen partridges dump their eggs in the nests of other female partridges who hatch and rear them, oblivious to the fact that those chicks are not their own. We now know that various kinds of bird do this and we name this behaviour as 'brood parasitism', with the cuckoo being the most well known example. While such behaviour may make sense for the parasite bird as she no longer needs to spend her energies feeding her natural young, it can be detrimental both to the host bird and the host's own offspring. In the words of the prophet she may prove to be a fool.

The Swift & The Thrush

I cried like a swift or thrush, I moaned like a mourning dove.

Isaiah 38 verse 14

Even the stork in the sky knows her appointed seasons, and the dove, the swift and the thrush observe the time of their migration. But my people do not know the requirements of the Lord.

Jeremiah 8 verse 7

Here are two identified kinds of birds which I have coupled together as they are mentioned in the same two biblical references and nowhere else in scripture. The first of these references was part of a personal letter written by King Hezekiah after his illness and recovery. In his letter he recounted his despair, fearing that he would die, and he wrote of crying like these birds. I find the king's linkage curious as the sounds these birds make differ considerably. Mention of a thrush crying is understandable as this bird typically has a loud, clear and indeed melodic voice, but the reference to the swift is intriguing. The main kind of swifts seen in modern Israel are also vocal and make soft yet shrill screaming sounds. Did the king recall making similar screams? The second reference is an extract from a lengthy commentary by the prophet Jeremiah about God's judgement on the people of Judah. The prophet contrasted the behaviour of migratory birds that know when it's the time for them to take action, including the swift and the thrush, with that of rebellious people who should have known their need to repent and obey God's laws.

The Ibis

Who gives the ibis wisdom or gives the rooster understanding?

Job 38 verse 36

Here is the only explicit reference to the ibis in the NIV Bible translation and it is a very positive one. After listening to Job's complaints and Elihu's long speech, the Lord asked Job a series of questions that served as a reminder of how creation in its many aspects points to God's sovereignty and power. Those questions began with a focus on various aspects of inanimate creation such as light, the weather and the stars, but moved on to focus on birds and animals. The first mentioned was the ibis, identified in Job as a bird given "wisdom". The accompanying footnote in the NIV Bible states that both the ibis and the rooster were birds "whose habits were observed by people to forecast the weather".

'Unclean' Birds

These are the birds you are to regard as unclean and not eat because they are unclean: the eagle, the vulture, the black vulture, the red kite, any kind of black kite, any kind of raven, the horned owl, the screech owl, the gull, any kind of hawk, the little owl, the cormorant, the great owl, the white owl, the desert owl, the osprey, the stork, any kind of heron, the hoopoe and the bat.

Leviticus 11 verses 13-19

You may eat any clean bird. But these you may not eat: the eagle, the vulture, the black vulture, the red kite, the black kite, any kind of falcon, any kind of raven, the horned owl, the screech owl, the gull, any kind of hawk, the little owl, the great owl, the white owl, the desert owl, the osprey, the cormorant, the stork, any kind of heron, the hoopoe and the bat.

Deuteronomy 14 verses 11-18

These two parallel lists of birds prohibited for consumption are virtually identical. Leviticus makes mention of "any kind of black kite" and the list in Deuteronomy adds ""any kind of falcon". Otherwise, the only difference in the lists themselves is to do with the sequencing of the cormorant.

Six kinds of bird are recorded in these lists that appear nowhere else in the Bible: the kite, gull, osprey, cormorant, heron and hoopoe. (Curiously, the bat is also mentioned as the final entry among the birds, although we now know it's not a kind of bird). The kite is identified as being of at least two forms – the red and the black – but the Leviticus reference also infers more than one kind of black kite. Intriguingly there is a variant kind of black kite in the biblical lands today – the yellow-billed kite currently found in Egypt.

The comparative table overlead illustrates how some translations of the Bible record a number of different birds in their parallel lists. The seventeenth-century King James Version in particular shows the most variance with seven kinds of bird not listed by the NIV: the ossifrage, nighthawk, cuckoo, swan, pelican, gier eagle and lapwing. I won't attempt to explain why there are such differences between translations, but the task of specific bird identification is clearly difficult to achieve when its only reference is a name on a list. The preface in my NIV Study Bible includes a statement from 'The Committee on Bible Translation' noting that "references to flora and fauna... cannot always be identified with precision".

Birds Listed as 'unclean' in Leviticus Chapter 11

ORDER NUMBER IN *NIV*	*NEW INTERNATIONAL VERSION* (PUBL. 1979)	PHONETIC HEBREW	*KING JAMES* (PUBL. 1611)	*JERUSALEM BIBLE*	*NEW REVISED STANDARD* (PUBL. 1990)
1	Eagle	*nesher*	eagle	tawny vulture	eagle
2	Vulture	*peres*	ossifrage	griffon	vulture
3	Black Vulture	*ozniyyah*	osprey	osprey	osprey
4	Red Kite	*da'ah*	vulture	kite	buzzard
5	Black Kite	*ayyah*	kite	several buzzards	kite
6	Raven	*oreb*	raven	raven	raven
7	Horned Owl	*ya'annah*	owl	ostrich	ostrich
8	Screech Owl	*tachmas*	nighthawk	screech owl	nighthawk
9	Gull	*sharaf*	cuckoo	seagull	seagull
10	Hawk	*nez*	hawk	several hawks	hawk
11	Little Owl	*kos*	little owl	horned owl	little owl
12	Cormorant	*shalak*	cormorant	cormorant	cormorant
13	Great Owl	*yanshuf*	great owl	barn owl	great owl
14	White Owl	*tinshemeth*	swan	ibis	water-hen
15	Desert Owl	*ka'ath*	pelican	pelican	desert-owl
16	Osprey	*rahama*	gier eagle	white vulture	carrion vulture
17	Stork	*hasidah*	stork	stork	stork
18	Herons	*anafah*	heron	several herons	heron
19	Hoopoe	*dukifath*	lapwing	hoopoe	hoopoe

Why were any of these birds listed? The Israelites were prohibited to eat any creature that killed others or ate dead flesh as part of a wider ban on eating animal blood that dated back to God's covenant with Noah after the Flood. We read in Genesis 9 that God blessed Noah and told him that he could supplement his diet with meat, but not with meat that "has its lifeblood still in it". Life was God's precious, sacred gift and blood was its God given life-force. As such it was not a substance to be consumed by people as a means of increasing the life-force in them. Hence the eating of blood would be prohibited under Mosaic law with strict procedures about draining out the blood of creatures killed to be eaten. All the birds listed as 'unclean' are either birds that kill or eat carrion in some undiscriminating form. Birds like the osprey, heron and the cormorant kill fish to eat, whereas the kite, gull and stork are examples of birds that can eat carrion. Even the hoopoe as an indiscriminate eater of muck and rubbish may eat carrion on occasion.

Perhaps a more obvious question today would be about omissions from the list. Why were some birds that kill not included such as the kingfisher, the tern or the shrike? Although these birds occur in modern Israel and Sinai, I presume they were not found then in sufficient numbers to be identified as possible sources of food. However, I am merely speculating.

Questions to Consider

1. Can we learn anything about God from the ostrich?

2. Why did the women of Zechariah's vision have the wings of storks?

3. What are the reasons why the Bible does not feature some kinds of larger birds like ducks that are found in modern Israel?

4. Are there any kinds of birds we should not eat today?

Unidentified Birds

There are plenty of biblical references to birds that are not identified as particular kinds or species. The precise number of these references is contested and I have not tried to calculate the total. [32] Nevertheless, there are many and they are found in the Old Testament across a wide range of scriptures including the Law, the Prophets, the Psalms and the historical narratives. There are also New Testament references that include the parables of Jesus, some epistles and the book of Revelation. They mainly relate to birds in general and they are diverse in terms of their imagery and subject matter, although a large percentage describe birds as agents of divine judgement. Here is a selection that is generally representative. I have grouped these references in terms of chronology where possible, beginning with the creation story in Genesis.

Creation

Now the earth was formless and empty, darkness was over the surface of the deep, and the Spirit of God was hovering over the waters.

Genesis 1 verse 2

In the second verse of the Bible the Spirit of God is described as "hovering over the waters". Although no bird is mentioned, many biblical commentators regard this as an avian allusion, i.e. that the Spirit was behaving like a bird. A subsequent link is made in the Bible between the Holy Spirit and a dove as we read in chapter 2, but the identity of a hovering bird is not at all obvious. Various kinds of birds can hover, like the eagle as Moses sang about in Deuteronomy 32, but fewer do so over water. Those that do are typically hunting for fish - birds like the osprey, tern and kingfisher. What a lovely speculative thought - the Spirit of God as a Kingfisher!

And God said, "Let the water teem with living creatures, and let birds fly over the earth across the vault of the sky."

Genesis 1 verse 20

The first explicit reference to birds is still found in the Bible's first chapter. In the creation narrative God created birds on the fifth day, i.e. in the same 'period' that he created sea creatures, and he created them to fly in the sky.

The phrase "the birds of the air", as used by Jesus in Matthew chapter 6, emphasises the point that the sky is the natural domain to which flying birds belong. Note too that birds were created before the animals "that move along the ground".

Then God said, "Let us make mankind in our image, in our likeness, so that they may rule over the fish in the sea and the birds in the sky, over the livestock and all the wild animals, and over all the creatures that move along the ground." So God created mankind in his own image, in the image of God he created them; male and female he created them. God blessed them and said to them, "Be fruitful and increase in number; fill the earth and subdue it. Rule over the fish in the sea and the birds in the sky and over every living creature that moves on the ground."

Genesis 1 verses 26-28

On the sixth day of the creation narrative God created human beings who would 'rule' over all other living creatures. They were made as different, to reflect the divine image. Precisely what is meant by being made "in the image of God" has been a matter of debate and contention, but it apparently includes humans acting as God's agents with delegated sovereignty to 'rule' over the natural world including "the birds in the sky". The NIV translation mentions mankind being made "in our image". Does this suggest that God is plural, or that God was addressing other heavenly beings, or does it perhaps hint at God's Trinitarian nature?

In recent years this passage has been identified as one of the most controversial in the Bible because of the subsequent and tragic history of human rule over other animals. Many critics have argued that the notion of people having a divine mandate to 'rule' over the natural world and 'subdue the earth' has led directly to enormous human misuse and abuse of nature. Some environmentalists and green activists claim that Judaeo-Christianity has been responsible for a mindset in Europe and North America that has legitimised habitat destruction, animal exterminations and even climate change, pointing to biblical texts like this as the source of the problem. Christians counter that 'ruling' and 'subduing' does not mean humankind has the right to dominate and destroy other animals and plants. We would argue instead that people have a God-given task to be stewards of the natural world with responsibility for its wellbeing.

Now the Lord God had formed out of the ground all the wild animals and all the birds in the sky. He brought them to the man to see what he would name them; and whatever the man called each living creature, that was its name. So the man gave names to all the livestock, the birds in the sky and all the wild animals.

Genesis 2 verse 19, 20

In the creation account of Genesis 2, the Lord God expressed concern about the man being alone and said he would find him a companion and helper, apparently from the living creatures he had already made. In the verses above we read that God brought these creatures to the man and asked him to name each one including each of the birds. None was a suitable helper for the man and the Lord God instead made a woman to be the man's companion. Hence we learn that "naming the creatures" was a duty given by God to humankind and a facet of our stewardship. I suggest that giving a creature a name implicitly requires us to take some responsibility for that creature... part of our 'creation care'.

Genesis Continued

The Genesis narrative continues with the account of the Fall, Noah and the Flood, Abraham and the ancestors of Israel, culminating with Joseph. Birds feature throughout the book, particularly in the story of Noah.

The Lord then said to Noah, "Go into the ark, you and your whole family, because I have found you righteous in this generation. Take with you seven pairs of every kind of clean animal, a male and its mate, and one pair of every kind of unclean animal, a male and its mate, and also seven pairs of every kind of bird, male and female, to keep their various kinds alive throughout the earth."

Genesis 7 verses 1–3

Noah was told to take into the ark seven pairs of every kind of bird, although the account goes on to suggest that he took only one pair of each (see chapter 7 verses 8 and 15). Two kinds of identified birds (the raven and the dove) were subsequently used by Noah to determine if the floodwaters had receded sufficiently.

When the chief baker saw that Joseph had given a favourable interpretation, he said to Joseph, "I too had a dream: On my head were three baskets of bread. In the top basket were all kinds of baked goods for Pharaoh, but the birds were eating them out of the basket on my head." "This is what it means," Joseph said. "The three baskets are three days. Within three days Pharaoh will lift off your head and impale your body on a pole. And the birds will eat away your flesh."

Genesis 40 verses 16-19

The story of Joseph includes a chilling tale of a dream with a sinister meaning. When Joseph was being held in prison in Egypt he was briefly joined by two royal officials. Each had a mysterious dream on the same night and neither knew what their dreams signified. The first, Pharaoh's cupbearer, recounted his dream to Joseph who gave a favourable interpretation in predicting that the official would soon be released and restored to his former position. Encouraged by Joseph's words, the second official then recounted his dream, but in stark contrast Joseph gave him a horrifying explanation which proved to be tragically accurate for that baker. Neither the kind of birds seen in the dream nor their numbers were apparently recalled, but the symbolism of these birds eating the baker's bread as a metaphor for his death was clear to Joseph.

The Law

We have already seen in Mosaic Law how specific kinds of birds were identified for sacrifice while others were deemed 'unclean' and banned from being eaten. Yet the Law also provided wider protection for breeding birds.

> *If you come across a bird's nest beside the road, either in a tree or on the ground, and the mother is sitting on the young or on the eggs, do not take the mother with the young. You may take the young, but be sure to let the mother go, so that it may go well with you and you may have a long life.*
>
> Deuteronomy 22 verse 6, 7

One of the Mosaic commands in an eclectic series of laws grouped together in chapter 22. It is presented immediately following a prohibition on transvestism and before a requirement to make roof parapets! Given that it was written over three thousand years ago, it is one of the oldest recorded laws on bird conservation. The simple message not to kill adult birds still makes sense to this day. Mother birds can reproduce eggs again and the birds as a kind will survive. Note the implicit threat the command contained if it was disobeyed – all would not go well with the transgressor.

Solomon & Wisdom Literature

King Solomon was credited with wisdom and wrote much

of the Bible's 'wisdom literature' including the Song of Songs, parts of Proverbs and perhaps the book of Ecclesiastes. His wisdom included a knowledge of birds as the historical narrative of 1 Kings explained.

He spoke about plant life, from the cedar of Lebanon to the hyssop that grows out of walls. He also spoke about animals and birds, reptiles and fish. From all nations people came to listen to Solomon's wisdom, sent by all the kings of the world, who had heard of his wisdom.

1 Kings 4 verses 33, 34

The writer of 1 Kings extolled the wisdom of King Solomon and claimed that he was wiser than any of his contemporaries. It is interesting to note that such wisdom included the acquisition of knowledge about the natural world. He learned and taught about the birds - an example that we might do so too.

Moreover, no one knows when their hour will come: As fish are caught in a cruel net, or birds are taken in a snare, so people are trapped by evil times that fall unexpectedly upon them.

Ecclesiastes 9 verse 12

Wise words from the author of Ecclesiastes. He reflected that none of us know when it's our time to die, and death may come like a sudden entrapment similar to the plight of birds caught in a snare.

The Psalms

The Psalms contain many references both to specific kinds of birds and to unidentified birds in general. These begin with Psalm 8 and end with Psalm 148 for which the relevant verses are shown below. In particular the psalms speak of God providing protection like a parent bird guarding its young under its wings and also of birds alongside other creatures praising God.

In the Lord I take refuge. How then can you say to me: "Flee like a bird to your mountain."

Psalm 11 verse 1

King David, the psalmist in this instance, declared his trust in God's protection and intention to stay put, unlike his advisers who were urging him to leave Jerusalem. The avian metaphor is of a bird fleeing away from hunters to the safety of the mountains.

I know every bird in the mountains, and the insects in the fields are mine.

Psalm 50 verse 11

A psalm of Asaph, one of King David's choir leaders, in which he addressed the people of Israel on God's behalf, rebuking them for their false understanding of sacrifice and their intentional evil behaviour. According to the psalmist, Israel's failure was not a lack of animal sacrifice, but of obeying God's covenant laws. All creatures including the birds were

144

already known and belonged to God who had no intrinsic need nor desire for their ritual killing.

He will cover you with his feathers, and under his wings you will find refuge; his faithfulness will be your shield and rampart.

Psalm 91 verse 4

A wonderful promise from a psalmist who was claiming the Lord God to be like a protective parent bird providing a safe refuge for those that place their trust in him. It contains similar sentiment to verse 8 in Psalm 17, verse 4 in Psalm 61 and verse 7 in Psalm 63. Did Jesus have such words in mind when he expressed his wish to be like a mother hen who could protect her young?

Praise the Lord from the earth, you great sea creatures and all ocean depths.... wild animals and all cattle, small creatures and flying birds....

Psalm 148 verse 7, 10

A song of praise from a psalmist who called on all of creation, animate and inanimate, to "praise the name of the Lord". Flying birds were invited to join in that chorus of praise alongside land-based animals and sea creatures, the weather elements, the mountains and hills, the trees and all people.

The Prophets

Most of the books of the Prophets mention birds. All five books of the major prophets (Isaiah, Jeremiah, Lamentations, Ezekiel and Daniel) have avian references, as do nine of the twelve books of the minor prophets. Only Jonah, Haggai and Malachi are devoid of birds. In the Prophets birds often feature as agents of God's judgement as we read in the examples from Ezekiel and Amos below. Yet there are tender references too about God's protection as we see in Isaiah.

Like birds hovering overhead, the Lord Almighty will shield Jerusalem; he will shield it and deliver it, he will 'pass over' it and will rescue it.

Isaiah 31 verse 5

Another reference to God being like a protective bird and its sentiment echoes the Song of Moses. The connection with the patriarch is made all the clearer with the mention of Israelite rescue when God 'passed over' their houses on the night that they fled Egypt. Although no kind of bird is specified, it was probable that the prophet Isaiah had eagles in mind.

I will leave you in the desert, you and all the fish of your streams. You will fall on the open field and not be gathered or picked up. I will give you as food to the beasts of the earth and the birds of the sky.

Ezekiel 29 verse 5

One of many biblical references to birds eating the bodies of people as part of divine punishment. In this case Ezekiel was prophesying judgment against Egypt, but similar warnings were given by other prophets against disobedient Jewish rulers and their rebellious people. Read the prophecies of Ahijah, Jehu and Elijah in 1 Kings 14, 16 and 21 respectively or Jeremiah's prophecies in chapters 7, 16 and 19 of the book that bears his name.

Does a bird swoop down to a trap on the ground when no bait is there? Does a trap spring up from the ground if it has not caught anything?

Amos 3 verse 5

Questions posed by Amos as he announced divine judgement on the Israelites. These words were part of a series of 'cause and effect' scenes drawn from daily life that were presented by the prophet as he developed God's case for bringing punishment on his sinful people. A bird wouldn't enter a trap without the incentive of bait nor would a trap be activated without something to catch. We can presume that people in the region at that time used snares and other traps to catch birds.

The Gospels

Jesus told us to watch birds and he talked about them. As well as the birds he specified like the vulture and the raven, Jesus also spoke about birds without identifying them in his stories.

> *Then he told them many things in parables, saying: "A farmer went to sow his seed. As he was scattering the seed, some fell along the path, and the birds came and ate it up."*

Matthew 13 verses 3, 4

Jesus talked about birds in two of his parables. The parable of the sower is probably the most well known and in which he described birds eating the sown seed that fell along the path. Jesus later explained to his disciples that these birds represented the devil, as they took away the word of God represented by the seed from the people who heard God's message but did not believe. Birds also featured in the parable of the Mustard Seed which grew from the smallest of seeds to become so large as a tree that birds could perch in its branches.

Acts, Epistles & Revelation

The remainder of the New Testament contains few references to birds. Paul's many letters contain only single references in Romans and 1 Corinthians, while neither John nor Peter mention them in their letters. It is interesting to ask why. Is it because the epistles were written for urban-based Christian churches operating in contexts where bird metaphors might seem less relevant? Only the book of Revelation has multiple avian references including the reference from chapter 19 - the last in the Bible.

Starting from the beginning, Peter told them the whole story: "I was in the city of Joppa praying, and in a trance I saw a vision. I saw something like a large sheet being let down from heaven by its four corners, and it came down to where I was. I looked into it and saw four-footed animals of the earth, wild beasts, reptiles and birds. Then I heard a voice telling me, 'Get up, Peter. Kill and eat'. I replied , 'Surely not, Lord! Nothing impure or unclean has ever entered my mouth.' The voice spoke from heaven a second time, 'Do not call anything impure that God has made clean'"

Acts 11 verses 4-9

In this passage Peter was recounting to Jewish Christians in Jerusalem the strange apparition he saw immediately prior to the arrival of a delegation from a Roman centurion. That timing evidently led Peter to interpret his vision as a God-given message about proclaiming the Gospel to 'unclean' Gentiles as well as the Jews, although he clearly struggled with the radical implications of that message later in life as revealed by his confrontation with Paul in Antioch (described in Galatians 2). It is unsurprising that a respectable Jew like Peter, brought up to obey Mosaic laws, would have been aghast at the very idea of knowingly eating foods deemed to be 'unclean ' that defile the body. Peter did not reveal the identity either of the 'unclean' birds or of the various other creatures lowered inside that sheet.

For although they knew God, they neither glorified him as God

149

nor gave thanks to him, but their thinking became futile and their foolish hearts were darkened. Although they claimed to be wise, they became fools and exchanged the glory of the immortal God for images made to look like a mortal human being and birds and animals and reptiles.

Romans 1 verses 21–23

An extract from Paul's material on God's righteousness and human sinfulness in his letter to Roman Christians. He argued that God's eternal power and divine nature were clear for all to see, yet people chose to reject him and instead to worship idols of their own making. These included images of birds as well as other living creatures.

All kinds of animals, birds, reptiles and sea creatures are being tamed and have been tamed by mankind, but no human being can tame the tongue. It is a restless evil, full of deadly poison.

James 3 verses 7, 8

A passing reference to birds by a Christian leader who was probably a blood half-brother of Jesus himself. The writer's strong comments contrasted humankind's ability to domesticate wild creatures including birds with our failure to curb our tongues and desist from speaking ill of others. His comments about animals and birds being tamed are fully understandable in view of farming experience by that time of keeping cattle, sheep, goats and chickens. However, it is much less apparent which examples of tame reptiles and sea creatures James had in mind.

And I saw an angel standing in the sun, who cried in a loud voice to all the birds flying in midair, "Come, gather together for the great supper of God, so that you may eat the flesh of kings, generals and the mighty, of horses and their riders, and the flesh of all people, free and slave, great and small." ....The rest were killed with the sword coming out of the mouth of the rider on the horse, and all the birds gorged themselves on their flesh.

Revelation 19 verses 17, 18 and 21

The final reference to birds in the Bible is found in its last book. It's another gory reference to God's judgement as St John in his vision saw an angel inviting all the birds to feast on the dead bodies of the kings of the earth and their armies.

Questions To Consider

1. What kind of bird could you imagine the hovering Spirit of God to be like?

2. Did Solomon's knowledge about birds really demonstrate his wisdom?

3. Are you reassured by the psalmist that God will cover you with his feathers?

4. Why is the Bible's last reference to birds about gory judgement?

And Finally ...

I have saved the best until last. Pardon the pun, but those of you with 'eagle eyes' may realise and been surprised that one kind of bird has so far not been discussed, although those with even keener eyes will already have spotted two biblical references to this bird in a previous chapter. I am of course writing about the sparrow. When I ask people which are the most featured birds in the Bible, many identify the sparrow and often name it first. It's not part of the leading quintet, but its five references make it eighth and it's only one of five kinds of birds to be mentioned specifically by Jesus.

Even the sparrow has found a home, and the swallow a nest for herself, where she may have her young - a place near your altar....

Psalm 84 verse 3

Like a fluttering sparrow or a darting swallow, an undeserved curse does not come to rest.

Proverbs 26 verse 2

They will come from Egypt, trembling like sparrows....

Hosea 11 verse 11

These Old Testament verses are based on observation. In each case the writer has noticed certain aspects of sparrow and swallow activity. The psalmist noted that both kinds of bird nest around buildings and observed they could still fly and enter the temple, whereas he was denied access. He yearned to return and envied the birds being able to nest inside God's house. The writer of the proverb considered the flight behaviour of each bird and noted their constant movement. It's easy today to watch a swallow flying and understand what was meant about it darting and not coming to rest, but the comment about a sparrow fluttering is less clear to me. My personal observations of bird fluttering relate only to very young birds of various species across the passerine family - fledglings who flutter their undeveloped wings continuously when their parents are feeding them. The same holds true for me about sparrows 'trembling'. Unlike the prophet, it's not a phenomenon I have knowingly witnessed.

Are not two sparrows sold for a penny? Yet not one of them will fall to the ground outside your Father's care. And even the very hairs of your head are all numbered. So don't be afraid; you are worth more than many sparrows.

Matthew 10 verses 29-31

Are not five sparrows sold for two pennies? Yet not one of them is forgotten by God. Indeed, the very hairs on your head are all numbered. Don't be afraid: you are worth more than many sparrows.

Luke 12 verses 6 and 7

The two Gospel references might relate to different occasions when Jesus was talking, but the core message was one and the same - "Don't be afraid". Theologian Tom Wright claims that this is the most repeated command in the Bible, and it was central to the teaching of Jesus.[33] Both Gospel writers set the verses above in the contexts of warnings Jesus gave to his followers that they would experience hostility. Nevertheless, he encouraged them not to be afraid as the misdeeds of their opponents would be exposed. Jesus reassured his followers that God their heavenly father loved them even more than the small birds being sold in the marketplace. It's probable that sparrows were abundant in Palestine at the time and so much part of the landscape that people didn't even notice them. Yet God remembers each and every sparrow, as Jesus said, so you have nothing to fear in God's love.

Why were sparrows being sold at the time of Jesus? Neither reference offers an explanation, but it seems sparrows were as 'cheap as chips' to buy. They were not listed among the 'unclean' birds in Leviticus and Deuteronomy, and presumably could be killed and eaten without violating Mosaic laws. Some commentators have suggested that sparrows were sold for sacrifice as even cheaper alternatives to buying pigeon-doves. I find that unlikely. No mention is made in the books of the Law about sacrificing sparrows and I suggest their small size would make them less malleable for dividing and blood draining in accordance with the sacrificial requirements detailed for example in Leviticus chapter 5. I suggest instead that sparrows were sold as a very cheap source of food – a practice that continues to this day in poor countries like Vietnam. I would speculate that catching small birds like sparrows was an option for very poor people with little other means of earning money. Make a net, build a simple wooden cage and go trapping sparrows to sell in the marketplace.

There is a deeper point here about God's attitude towards creation being very different to ours. We might not value the sparrows that are sold in the market for pennies, but Jesus clearly said that God values them and notes the death of each one. Sparrows are creatures of God, loved by Him in their own right and not because of our relationship with them. Yet by contrast it seems that we as people typically view birds like sparrows, animals, plants and indeed the planet as utilitarian objects that we value only in terms of their use to us. Consider the ways we continue to kill animals cruelly, subject them to experiment for commercial purposes, destroy their habitats and drive them to extinction. We are subjecting much of nature to 'biological annihilation' currently affecting thousands of species of animals and plants. Some scientists argue that there is a sixth mass extinction of wildlife taking place today, similar in scale to the extinctions of the past that killed off the dinosaurs. [34] However, the difference is that this annihilation is largely human-made - a result of our activities in causing habitat loss and global warming. How does that square with our responsibilities to be God's stewards of creation?

A well known twentieth-century hymn takes these words of Jesus as its theme. In 1905 a songwriter, Civilla Martin, wrote 'His Eye Is on the Sparrow' after visiting a bedridden friend in New York state. Her friend, Mrs Doolittle, had explained how she stayed so positive despite her chronically poor physical health: "Mrs Martin, how can I be discouraged when my heavenly Father watches over each little sparrow and I know he loves and cares for me?"[35] That expression of faith inspired Civilla Martin to write the hymn, and during the century it became a favourite with Gospel singers. The list of famous artists who have recorded it reads like a who's who: Mahalia Jackson in 1956; Marvyn Gaye in 1968; Gladys Knight in 2009 at the funeral service of Michael Jackson, and Whitney Houston in 2012 - her version being released posthumously as a single.

A similar sentiment was expressed by the Christian writer,

Joni Eareckson Tada, at a time when she was confined to her bed and watching the birds on the feeder outside her window:

> *I glanced at the bird feeder and smiled. I could understand Jesus noticing an eagle... But a scrappy sparrow? They're a dime a dozen. Jesus said so himself. Yet from thousands of bird species the Lord chose the most insignificant, least-noticed scruffiest bird of all. A pint-sized thing that even dedicated birdwatchers ignore. That thought alone calmed my fears. I felt significant and noticed.... If the great God of heaven concerns himself with a ragtag little sparrow clinging to the bird feeder outside my window, he cares about you.*[36]

Not all Christians have shown such concern for sparrows. In August 1979 the death of a sparrow in England became international news. A House Sparrow got trapped inside a Lincolnshire village church and broke into song during a classical guitar recital being recorded for a BBC Radio 3 broadcast. The vicar asked the congregation to leave, summoned a marksman with an air gun, and had the bird shot. The killing of this sparrow became a news item in Britain and America with headline writers poking fun at the cleric's forename. One such was the Daily Telegraph newspaper which ran the headline that 'Rev. Robin orders death of sparrow.' Editorials and public opinion strongly condemned the act and reminded readers of the reference from Psalm 84. Only two days after that incident I was travelling on a bus through London when I saw a church poster that grabbed my attention. It simply featured two words that were printed large: 'SPARROWS WELCOME!' I smiled. Someone at that church clearly understood what Jesus meant

I thought, unlike the village vicar.

Even sparrows are loved by God. That's why I use the term 'Even Sparrows' as the name for my organisation and a sparrow picture as its logo. Yet that picture tells a story. It's of a Tree Sparrow, a bird that was once common in the British countryside. However, the population crashed by more than 90% between the late 1970s and the 1990s with the species disappearing in many parts of Britain.[37] The reasons for this dramatic decline are not entirely clear, but it seems likely that intensive farming and the wider use of herbicides have been contributory factors. Thankfully, Tree Sparrow numbers are now increasing, although the overall population is much lower than a half century ago. Their plight serves as a salutary warning – that birds and other animals we consider common can plummet in numbers due to human activities, however unintended. Yet if God even loves sparrows, we surely have a duty of care to protect our wildlife and prevent such crashes from happening in future.

Let's return to those opening words from Jesus to "look at the birds of the air". The Greek word used in Matthew 6 verse 26 is transliterated as *emblepo* – defined as 'looking attentively' or 'searchingly'. There is an intensity and purpose implied about the looking. It is an act requiring full focus and deliberation. It's not an activity that you undertake casually with your mind half concentrating on something else. I find it interesting to note that the same Greek word is used ten times across the Gospels, primarily for occasions when Jesus was looking intently at people. In Mark chapter 11 it's the word used to describe Jesus looking at the rich young ruler when he told him to sell his possessions and give to the poor. In John chapter 1 it's the word recorded when Jesus looked at a fisherman named Simon and re-named him Peter as he welcomed him as a disciple. Poignantly in Luke chapter 22 it's the verb employed for the moment in the courtyard when the rooster crowed and Jesus turned to look at that very same man who had thrice denied knowing him.

'Look and learn'. It was the title of a children's magazine which I read as a boy in the 1960s. I don't remember much about the content, but the catchy title has always stayed with me. Three short words and a straightforward instruction. It's the same command Jesus gave his followers in Matthew 6. Let's look at birds and learn about God's love.

Look at the Birds of the Air

Notes

1. Christians remain divided over the 'creation v evolution' debate and I should declare my position. I do so with reluctance, knowing that I might offend some Christians who feel compelled to dismiss my arguments because they may deem that position to be 'unsound'. Although I write as a Christian who claims to accept biblical authority, I do not share in a belief that the universe was created in six consecutive periods of twenty-four hours as the literal interpretation of Genesis chapter 1 seems to require, nor do I believe that Noah's flood engulfed the entire earth. What I dispute most is the idea expressed by some 'creationists' that God created animals including birds in distinct and different categories that have remained fixed ever since. Darwin's theories of evolution developed as a result of studying birds and I can understand why.

2. Birkhead, T. *The Wisdom of Birds.* 2008. Bloomsbury, London, page 305.

3. I have used the official Israeli 'Birding Website' as my source about the current status of particular wild birds in modern Israel. The website is run by members of the Israeli Rarities and Distribution Committee, and in June 2018 its home page was claiming that 500 million birds pass through the country each spring and autumn.
Accessed on 5 June 2018 from http://www.israbirding.com/

4. Cocker, M. and Mabey, R. *Birds Britannica*. Chatto & Windus, London, page 262.

5. These descriptive words about the eagle are uttered by Sicilius Leonatus in Act 5, Scene 4.

6. Lord Tennyson, A. 'The Eagle'. *Selected Poems*. 2007. Gramercy Books, New York, page 70.

7. Curran, E. 'The Eagle'.
Accessed on 5 June 2018 from www.blackcatpoems.com/c/the eagle

8. Debbie Blue is among those who think the thunderbird legends are based on the eagle. See Blue, D. *Consider the Birds*. 2013. Abingdon Press, Nashville, page 86.

9. Accessed on 5 June 2018 from https://www.statista.com/statistics/263962/number-of-chickens-worldwide-since-1990/

10. See the feature article 'How Poultry Performed Globally in 2016 - and What to expect in 2017' from the Poultry Site website.
Accessed on 5 June 2018 from
http://www.thepoultrysite.com/articles/3681/how-poultry-performed-globally-in-2016-and-what-to-expect-in-2017/

11. My calculation is based on the statistic that the average live weight of a chicken at slaughter is 2.2kg. That converts to a 'dressing out' percentage of 73%, hence the meat of a dead bird weighs 1.65kg. Divide 115.8 million metric tonnes by 1.65 kg and you arrive at a figure of 70.2 million million birds – FAR in excess of the 22 billion birds I quote at the start of the chapter. Is this a case of "lies, damn lies and statistics"?!

12. See the WATT Executive Guide to World Poultry Trends 2017, page 30.
Accessed on 5 June 2018 from
http://www.poultrytrends.com/201711/index.php#/32/

13. Cocker, M. and Tipling, D. *Birds and People*. 2012. Jonathan Cape, London, page 64.

14. See the Breed Gallery page of the Poultry Club of Great Britain website.
Accessed on 5 June 2018 from
http://www.poultryclub.org/breed-gallery/

15. My estimates of Israeli consumption of eggs and chicken meat are based on statistics from the article 'Israeli poultry going for a new reform' in Poultry World on 28 September 2009.
Accessed on 5 June 2018 from
https://www.poultryworld.net/Breeders/General/2009/9/Israeli-poultry-going-for-a-new-reform-WP006954W/

16. See the news article by Sharon Udasin in the Jerusalem

Post on 1 October 2016.
Accessed on 5 June 2018 from
https://www.jpost.com/Business-and-Innovation/
Environment/Agriculture-Ministry-introduces-campaign-
against-kaparot-ritual-469249/

17. Lawler, A. and Adler, J. 'How the Chicken Conquered
the World', *Smithsonian Magazine*, June 2012.
Accessed on 5 June 2018 from
https://www.smithsonianmag.com/history/how-the-
chicken-conquered-the-world-87583657/

18. Cocker, M. and Tipling, D., op cit, page 66.

19. Trudgian, R. 'In Search of Biblical Birds' in Stromberg, L.
Poultry of the World. 1996. Silvio Mattacchione & Co, Ontario,
page 46.

20. Julian of Norwich. *Revelations of Divine Love*. 1966.
Penguin, London, page 168.

21. Unwin, M. and Tipling, D. *A Parliament of Owls*. 2016.
William Collins, London, page 19.

22. Unwin, M. and Tipling, D. op cit, page 168.

23. See 'Patoo', Petchary's blog for 5 April 2012
Accessed on 5 June 2018 from https://petchary.wordpress.
com/2012/04/05/patoo/

24. TRAFFIC is an NGO monitoring the global wildlife trade. In 2010 it published a report on the illicit trapping and trading of owls in India.
Accessed on 5 June 2018 from
http://www.traffic.org/home/2010/11/2/black-magic-behind-illegal-owl-trade-in-india.html/

25. See ' Owl Tales from Africa', a short narrative by Bruce Marcot of his field research among rural people in central and southern Africa.
Accessed on 5 June 2018 from
https://www.owlpages.com/owls/articles.php?a=64&p=3/

26. Accessed on 5 June 2018 from
http://news.bbc.co.uk/1/hi/world/africa/5275678.stm/

27. See the Facebook page for Naivasha Owl Centre.
Accessed on 5 June 2018 from
https://www.facebook.com/pg/naivashaowls/

28. See my blog, 'A curious owl'
Accessed on 5 June 2018 from
http://www.birdwatchnorthumbria.co.uk/blog/detail.php?id=28/

29. Quoted in Cocker, M. and Mabey, R. *Birds Britannica.* Chatto & Windus, London, page 423.

30. Ackerman, Jo. *The Genius of Birds.* 2016. Corsair, London, page 121.

31. McManners, J. *Cuthbert and the Animals.* Undated. Gemini Productions, page 41.

32. Some commentators like Alice Parmelee have recorded every mention of wings, nests, eggs and net traps as avian references. She even included references to the cherubim (the heavenly creatures first noted in Genesis 3) in her avian list on the basis of them being winged creatures.

33. Wright, T. *Matthew for Everyone* Part 1. 2002. SPCK, London, page 118.

34. Carrington, D. 'Earth's sixth mass extinction event under way, scientists warn'. The Guardian. 10 July 2017.
Accessed on 5 June 2018 from
https://www.theguardian.com/environment/2017/jul/10/earths-sixth-mass-extinction-event-already-underway-scientists-warn/

35. Quoted by David Padfield in the website article, 'His Eye Is On The Sparrow'
Accessed on 5 June 2018 from
https://hayticoc.com/wp/2017/07/25/his-eye-is-on-the-sparrow/

36. Taken from *When is it Right to Die? Suicide, Euthanasia,*

Suffering and Mercy by Joni Eareckson Tada, Zondervan, 1992, pp23-25, 178-9.

Used by permission of Zondervan. www.zondervan.com/

37. Accessed on 5 June 2018 from
https://www.bto.org/birdtrends2010/wcrtresp.shtml/

Bibliography

The following publications have been particularly helpful in writing this book and are recommended for further reading.

Ackerman, Jo. *The Genius of Birds*. 2016. Corsair, London.

Avery, M. *A Message from Martha*. 2014. Bloomsbury, London.

Birkhead, T. *The Wisdom of Birds*. 2008. Bloomsbury, London.

Birkhead, T. *Bird Sense*. 2012. Bloomsbury, London.

Blue, D. *Consider the Birds*. 2013. Abingdon Press, Nashville.

Cocker, M. and Mabey, R. *Birds Britannica*. 2005. Chatto & Windus, London.

Cocker, M. and Tipling, D. *Birds and People*. 2012. Jonathan Cape, London.

Delacour, J. *Wild pigeons and doves*. 1980. T.F.H., New Jersey.

Goodfellow, P. *Birds of the Bible*. 2013. John Beaufoy, Oxford.

Holmgren, V.C. *Bird Walk Through the Bible*. 1972. Seabury Press, New York.

McManners, J. *Cuthbert and the Animals*. Undated. Gemini

Productions.

Papworth, D. *The Lives Around Us*. 2015. John Hunt, Alresford.

Parmelee, A. *All the Birds of the Bible*. 1959. Lutterworth Press, London.

Snow, D. W. and Perrins, C.M. *The Birds of the Western Palearctic* Concise Edition. 1998. OUP, Oxford.

Stott, J. *The Birds Our Teachers*. 1999. Candle Books, London.

Stromberg, L. *Poultry of the World*. 1996. Silvio Mattacchione & Co, Ontario.

Svensson, L., Mullarney, K. and Zetterstrom, D. *Collins Bird Guide* 2nd Edition. 2009. Harper Collins, London.

Unwin, M. and Tipling, D. *A Parliament of Owls*. 2016. William Collins, London.

Watkins, P. and Stockland, J. *Winged Wonders*. 2005. Canterbury Press, Norwich.

Bird References of The Bible

Most Old Testament books have references, but New Testament references are largely confined to the Gospels and Revelation. All the key references are shown below.

GENESIS

Creation	1:2,20,21,22,26,28,30
	2:19,20
Noah	6:7,20
	7:3,8,14,21,23
	8:7-12,17,19,20
	9:2,10
Abraham	15:9-11
Joseph	40:17-19

THE EXODUS

Quails	Exodus 16:13
	Numbers 11:31,32
God speaks on Mt Sinai	Exodus 19:4
Balaam's final oracle	Numbers 24:21
Song of Moses	Deuteronomy 32:11

THE LAW

Bird idolatry forbidden	Deuteronomy 4:17
Birds as sacrifices	Leviticus 1:14-17
	5:7-11
	12:6-8
	14:22,30-31,49-53

	15:13–15,28–29
	Numbers 6:10
Prohibition on bird blood	Leviticus 7:26
	17:13
Taking birds' eggs	Deuteronomy 22: 6,7
Curses for Disobedience	Deuteronomy 28:26,49
'Unclean' birds	Leviticus 11:13–19,46
	20:25
	Deuteronomy 14:11–18,20

THE BOOKS OF HISTORY

David & Goliath	1 Samuel 17:44,46
David being hunted	1 Samuel 26:20
Saul & Jonathan	2 Samuel 1:23
Rizpah	2 Samuel 21:10
Solomon's daily provisions	1 Kings 4:23
Solomon's wisdom	1 Kings 4:33,34
Prophecies of birds eating bodies	1 Kings 14:11
	16:4
	21:24
Nehemiah's food for staff	Nehemiah 5:18

WISDOM LITERATURE

Job	9:26
	12:7
	15:23
	28:7,21
	30:29

	35:11
	38:36,41
	39:13-18,26-30
	41:5
Proverbs	6:5
	7:23
	23:5
	26:2
	27:8
	30:17,19, 29-31
Ecclesiastes	9:12
	10:20
	12:4
Song of Songs	1:15
	2:12,14
	4:1
	5:2,11,12
	6:9

PSALMS

8:8	11:1
50:11	55: 6
56:title	61:4
68:13	74:19
78:27	79:2
84:3	91:4
102:6,7	103:5
104:12,17	105:40
124:7	147:9

148:10

THE PROPHETS

Elijah	1 Kings 17:2-4,6	
	1 Kings 21: 24	
Isaiah	8:8	10:14
	13:21	14:23
	16:2	18:6
	31:5	34:11-15
	38:14	40:31
	43:20	46:11
	59:11	60:8
Jeremiah	4:13,25	5:26,27
	7:33	8:7
	9:10	12:4,9
	15:3	16:4
	17:11	19:7
	34:20	48:28,40
	49:16,22	50:39
Lamentations	3:52	
	4:3,19	
Ezekiel	1:10	7:16
	10:14	13:20
	17:1-7,23	29:5
	31:6,13	32:4
	38:20	39:4,17
	44:31	
Daniel	2:38	
	4:12,14,21,33	

	7:4,6
Hosea	2:18
	4:3
	7:11,12
	8:1
	9:11
	11:11,12
Amos	3:5
Obadiah	1:4
Micah	1:8,16
Nahum	2:7
Habakkuk	1:8
Zephaniah	1:3
	2:14
Zechariah	5:9

THE GOSPELS

Dedication of baby Jesus	Luke 2:24
Baptism of Jesus	Matthew 3:16
	Mark 1:10
	Luke 3:21,22
	John 1:32
Teaching of Jesus	Matthew 6:26
	10:29,31
	Luke 12:6,7,24
Cost of following Jesus	Matthew 8:20
	Luke 9:58
Sending out the Twelve	Matthew 10:16
Parable of Mustard Seed	Matthew 13:32

	Mark 4:32
	Luke 13:19
Parable of Sower	Matthew 13:4
	Mark 4:4
	Luke 8:5
Prophecy on Jerusalem	Matthew 23:37
	Luke 13:34
Second Coming Prophecy	Matthew 24:28
	Mark 13:35
	Luke 17:37
Clearing the Temple	Matthew 21:12
	Mark 11:15
	John 2: 14,16
Peter's denial	Matthew 26:34,74,75
	Mark 14:30,72
	Luke 22:34,60-61
	John 13:38 18:27

ACTS

Peter's vision	10:12
	11:6

ROMANS

Foolish idolatry	1:23

1 CORINTHIANS

Resurrection body	15:39

JAMES
Birds being tamed   3:7

REVELATION
Vision of 4 living creatures   4:7
Eagle crying "Woe!"   8:13
Woman & dragon   12:14
Babylon – haunt of 'unclean' birds   18:2
Invitation to the birds   19:17,21

Acknowledgements

Various friends have supported me in writing this book. In particular I want to thank Professor Charlotte Clarke and the Reverends David Archer, Dale Hanson, Adrian Hughes, Jenny Lancaster and Judith Sadler who were each willing to review early drafts. Their positive comments and constructive criticisms gave me the encouraging signal I needed to carry on, although I should add that I alone take full responsibility for the views expressed in my book. I am also thankful to Ian Allonby of the Poultry Club for a fascinating morning discussing chicken breeds and his kind loan of specialist books. And I owe big thanks to local artist and friend, Simon Terry, for his inspired cover design and chapter illustrations.

Above all, I am especially grateful for the loving and practical help from my family. Anna, our daughter, for her advice and continual support; Luke, our son, for his editing skills and guidance on self publishing; Sheila, as always, for her gentle and constant encouragement.

CPSIA information can be obtained
at www.ICGtesting.com
Printed in the USA
LVHW041638130423
744289LV00001B/155